Ghana *and the* Rawlings Factor

Kevin Shillington

M
MACMILLAN

First published 1992

Published by THE MACMILLAN PRESS LTD
London and Basingstoke
Associated companies and representatives in Accra, Auckland, Delhi, Dublin, Gaborone, Hamburg, Harare, Hong Kong, Kuala Lumpur, Lagos, Manzini, Melbourne, Mexico City, Nairobi, New York, Singapore, Tokyo.

ISBN 0–333–56840–0 (Pbk)
ISBN 0–333–56845–1 (Hbk)

Printed in Singapore

A catalogue record for this book is available from the British Library.

For the people of Ghana

Contents

Acknowledgements

I have incurred many debts in the writing of this book. I have interviewed a wide range of people of all political persuasions, from the Head of State and members of his government to opponents in political exile. All have been extremely generous with their time, assistance and hospitality. While acknowledging, however, that I have relied heavily for this book upon information learned through interview, and while I have made every endeavour to respect and represent the views, memories and opinions of my informants, I have checked and cross-checked all my information as far as possible and responsibility for any errors of fact, interpretation or emphasis must remain mine alone.

I should particularly like to thank the Chairman of the PNDC, Flight Lieutenant J.J.Rawlings, who granted me many hours of his time discussing events of the past, problems of the present and prospects for the future. He and members of his government spoke freely about their experiences and ideas. I am grateful to the following for the extensive interviews which they granted me : Justice Daniel F. Annan, PNDC member and Chairman of the NCD; P.V. Obeng, PNDC member and Chairman of the Committee of Secretaries; Captain Kojo Tsikata, PNDC member responsible for Security and Foreign Affairs; Dr Kwesi Botchwey, Secretary for Finance and Economic Planning; Kofi Totobi Quakye, Secretary for Information; Kwamena

Ahwoi, Secretary for Local Government; Joyce Aryee, Special Assistant to Justice Annan; Dr S.K.B.Asante, Chairman of the Committee of Experts on the Constitution; Sam Garba, Deputy Secretary for CDRs; and Tsatsu Tsikata, special adviser to the Chairman. I should like to thank Mr Totobi Quakye, in particular, for the assistance of his staff at the Ministry of Information; and Mr Kwamena Ahwoi for inviting me to accompany him on a tour of inspection of Ashanti Region. I am also extremely grateful to Mrs Agyeman Rawlings for the amount of information with which she entrusted me.

My thanks are similarly due to the following for their time and confidence in interview or for their help in other ways: His Excellency Dr J.L.S.Abbey, Ghana's Ambassador to the United States; His Excellency K.B.Asante, Ghana's High Commissioner to the United Kingdom; The Asantehene, Otumfuo Opoku Ware II; Dr Hilla Limann, President of the Third Republic; Right Reverend Peter Kwesi Sarpong, Bishop of Kumasi; Reverend Dr Samuel Asante Antwi, Chairman of the Methodist Church, Kumasi District; Miss Pauline Clerk and the officers of the National Council for Women in Development; Mr A.K.Yankey, Secretary General of the TUC; Mr Ako Adjei, 'the last of the Big Six'; Dr Gobin Nankani and Ernest Ako Adjei of the World Bank, Washington; the late Professor K.B. Dickson, Professor D.K.Agyeman, Dr Ata Britwum, Dr Jebouni, Dr K.A. Ninsin, Professor E.O.Asare, Dr F.K.Buah, Group Captain Frank Okyne, Ben Egan, Kofi Bentun Quantson, Robin Kibuka, George Yankey, Philip Giase, Kojo Yankah, Tesfay Teklu, S.A.Afreh, Christian Aggrey, Sam Clegg, Ajoa Yeboah-Afari, Sarah Pennington, Father Joop Visser, Father Ben Donkor, Father Charles Palmer Buckle, F.K.Chapman-Wardy, J.H.Mensah, Sam Okutzeto, Goosie Tanoh, Larry Ala Adjetey, Peter Ala Adjetey, Kofi Akumanyi, Kojo Botsio, Johnny Hansen, K. Gyan-Apenteng, Chris Bukari Atim, Zaya Yeebo, Stephen Ellis, Major K. Boakye Djan,

Elizabeth Ohene, Joe Bradford Nyinah, Kwamena Anaman, Kwesi Pratt, Robert Frimpong-Manfo, Warrant Officer Tetteh, Elvis Aryeh, Kofi Caesar, Bernard Abeiku Arthur, Maame Arhim, Rachel McCarthy, Comfort Ashitey, Mike Mensah, Tony Obeng, Mr Amamoo, and the cocoa farmers of Mankranso : Nana Kwame Anane Kesse, Nana Kwasi Gyan, Nana Kwasi Kwarteng, Joseph Adomako Aboatye, Nana Kofi Owusu, Kwabena Manu, Aduoa Manu, Amua Anto, Amua Bosuo and Amua Kyere. My thanks also to the few people who asked not to be mentioned by name. I am grateful to all those Ghanaians whose hospitality and help in so many ways made my two research visits to Ghana so enjoyable and productive.

In addition to the information and insights learned from personal informants, I consulted widely in books, articles, contemporary newspapers and numerous official and unofficial papers and reports. A list of some of the principal sources can be found near the end of the book.

Finally, I cannot end without a special word of thanks to Gloria for many hours spent transcribing tapes, to Shirley for her patience with the manuscript, and to Eddie and Emma, above all, for their friendship.

Kevin Shillington,
London, September 1991.

Prologue

1979 was a year of major change in Africa. It saw the felling of three of the continent's most corrupt and tyrannical regimes – that of Bokassa in the Central African Republic, Nguema in Equatorial Guinea and Amin in Uganda. In West Africa, a region long-disturbed by military intervention in national politics, a new trend was set in motion as the military rulers of both Nigeria and Ghana prepared to return power to civilian elected governments. As the war for independence in Zimbabwe entered its final phase, hopes were riding high for a new era of freedom and justice for all the peoples of Africa.

Suddenly, the attention of the international media was gripped with excitement as the name 'Jerry Rawlings' was flashed around the news wires of the world.

The place was Accra, capital of Ghana. The date was 4 June 1979.

In the early hours of that hot and sultry Monday morning, among the chaos of an unexpected and spontaneous *coup d'état*, a young Air Force Flight Lieutenant, on trial for his life on a charge of mutiny, was dramatically sprung from prison and proclaimed Head of State.

Flight Lieutenant Rawlings, Chairman of the newly-proclaimed Armed Forces Revolutionary Council, declared war against corruption. Hoarding of goods was outlawed and rock-bottom price controls were strictly enforced in all the country's major markets. But the main attention of the new regime was turned inwards on corruption among the military themselves. Before the month was out eight senior military officers, including three former Heads of State, had been executed by firing squad. Yet, incredibly, amid all the drama and apparent chaos of the time, parliamentary and presidential elections went ahead as planned and, barely three and a half months after his propulsion into office, Rawlings handed over power to the new civilian President, a week ahead of schedule.

As he resumed his place among the ranks on the parade ground that September day, there was little doubt among Ghanaians that Flight Lieutenant Rawlings had been the most wildly popular Head of State since Nkrumah in his earliest years. Whatever else might happen in the future, June 4th was firmly embedded in the Ghanaian psyche.

That, however, was only a beginning. Ghanaians were destined to witness a 'second coming'! Twenty-seven months after handing over office, Rawlings returned, seizing power again by force on 31 December 1981 and setting up a Provisional National Defence Council (PNDC). This time he came not merely to 'cleanse' the upper ranks of the military establishment, but to initiate a revolution.

For the third time in sixteen years Ghana's civilian republic was overthrown by a military *coup d'état*. Why? What set of circumstances had developed that should lead to such a swift collapse of the country's Third Republic? What was the 'Rawlings factor'; and what has been the nature of his 'revolution' in the intervening decade?

In order to understand the nature and underlying causes of events in 1979, which led to the revolution of 1981, one needs to go back to the roots of Ghanaian political instability, social dislocation and economic decline, and it is wise to look for these in the early years of Ghanaian independence.

Chapter 1

From Nkrumah to Akuffo, 1957–1979

Ghana in the early 1990s has reached a stage of development and transition, as critical in its own way as the achievement of independence in 1957. There is a sense of excitement and expectation in the air. Aspiring politicians see the PNDC government's moves towards a revival of party politics as a positive and exciting opportunity which has been denied them for the past ten years. On the other hand, there are very many Ghanaians whose hopes for the future are tinged with considerable anxiety. While there is an almost universal desire for a return to some form of constitutional government, many people worry whether such a transition can be safely achieved without losing the continuity of development and undoubted economic gains of the past decade.

Ghana's political history has known many new beginnings that have ultimately disappointed their initial expectations. Ghanaians of all political persuasions justly look back with pride to the late 1950s when Ghana, led by Kwame Nkrumah, became the first sub-Saharan African country to throw off the yoke of imperialism. But whatever happened to the inspiration and the promise of 1957? Dedicated 'Nkrumahists' blame all the nations's subsequent ills upon those external enemies and their internal lackeys who challenged and betrayed the Osagyefo's African revolution. Others, tempered by rather different memories, argue that it was the Osagyefo himself who betrayed his own revolution by riding roughshod over the nation's founding principles of 'Freedom and Justice' for all. A more dispassionate assessment of Nkrumah, however, must place his suppression of certain individual freedoms in the context of the undemocratic and often violent methods of those opponents who sought to undermine and even to overthrow his government. Ultimately, too, any fair assessment of the era would acknowledge the importance of Nkrumah's larger vision, for it embraced the future, not only of the nation, but of the continent as a whole. Unfortunately, the depth and long-term validity of Nkrumah's vision of a self-dependent Africa was appreciated by few of his contemporaries.

There can be no doubt that the achievements of the Nkrumah years, in terms of social and economic development, were immense. But while acknowledging those achievements, it is equally important to understand something of their limitations. For just as the foundations for Ghana's future development were laid in the decade and a half from 1951 to 1966, so too were the foundations laid for the conflict and decline that followed.

In those early years of independence Ghana was indeed 'The Black Star' of Africa. Ghana's route to independence through mass action on the streets combined with peaceful constitutional negotiation behind the scenes, had set the trend for other aspirant African leaders to emulate. After independence, Nkrumah was inspirational in the African struggle against the new economic imperialism which stretched far beyond the formal end of empire. His striving for economic self-reliance through some form of socialist central control of the economy laid the foundations for a new African economic order. Even those emergent African leaders who were philosophically firmly in the capitalist camp were influenced by Nkrumah's socialist rhetoric and many were envious of the extent of Ghana's apparent economic self-reliance.

Kwame Nkrumah's interests stretched way beyond the confines of his own country, Ghana. He was a Pan-Africanist of great vision and it is only now, a generation later, that Africans are gradually coming to appreciate the value of his concepts. Nkrumah looked at the example of the two great super powers of his day, the United States of America and the Soviet Union, and strove to steer a middle course of non-alignment between East and West. He saw that the only route to true African independence, economic as well as political, was through the creation of what he called 'a continental Union Government of Africa'. The continent had the human and physical resources to form an independent and self-sustaining union, it only required the political will to make it a reality. But Nkrumah's vision was way ahead of his time. The rulers of the newly emergent African states were more concerned with unity within their own borders and were not about to give up their new-found independence for the ideals of a visionary. Although Nkrumah was instrumental in founding the Organisation of African Unity (OAU) in 1963, the final product was a talking-shop, an ineffective and diluted compromise – a mere shadow of the Osagyefo's dream.

Nkrumah's place in the vast expanse of African history is assured, but it is on his record of government in his own country that he will be most closely and most critically judged, and it is here that his role is most important for the purposes of this book.

Nkrumah began his time in government as much as six years before independence. In 1951 his Convention People's Party (CPP) won an overwhelming majority of the thirty-eight elected seats in the new eighty-four member Legislative Assembly. Nkrumah, who was serving a prison sentence at the time for conducting a campaign of 'Positive Action' on the streets, was released from prison and invited by the colonial governor to become 'Leader of Government Business'. The following year his title was changed to that of 'Prime Minister' and although further constitutional changes and two more general elections were still to take place before independence, the CPP administration was now able to make a start upon its ambitious programme for social and economic development.

Nkrumah's social policy was guided by the ultimate aim of universal free education and health facilities, combined with high quality water and sanitation, affordable housing for all and wide access to electricity. Armed with these basic human rights, he believed, there would be no limit to the development prospects of Ghanaians.

The fifteen years from 1951 to 1966 was a time of constant construction and expansion. Hospitals were refurbished and new ones were constructed, culminating in the building of the Korle Bu Teaching Hospital where Ghana could train her own doctors. A project was embarked upon to provide potable water for all rural villages while concrete sewage drains were constructed in the towns. In the field of education there was rapid expansion in the numbers of both primary and secondary schools. Primary schools were increased from 1083 in 1951 to over 8000 by 1966 with places for more than a million pupils. By 1961 primary schooling with free tuition was universal and compulsory. Middle and secondary schools were similarly expanded, although more slowly. These achievements were crowned in the years before and after independence by numerous teacher training colleges and three universities.

In the field of economic policy Nkrumah's aims were equally far-reaching. Hitherto the economy of the colonial 'Gold Coast' had been based upon the export of raw materials, principally cocoa, gold and timber, to the developed world of Europe and North America. Not only were prices for these commodities determined in far-off financial centres such as London, but those same developed industrial economies set the prices for the manufactured consumer goods which the underdeveloped economy of the 'Gold Coast' was expected to import. In other words, the developed world dictated the terms of trade. In times of crisis in the developed world, commodity prices were reduced while those of manufactured goods remained constant or increased. This meant that a country like Ghana had to export more and more of her cocoa and her timber just in order to be able to import the same amount of manufactured goods: tractors, trucks, machinery, fertiliser, chemicals, clothing, books, household utensils and other essential consumer goods. In this way any economic weakness in the developed industrial world could be off-loaded onto the backs of African labour: not in so direct a manner as in the era of the slave trade, but nevertheless in a dependent relationship which Nkrumah was to label 'neo-colonialism'.

Determined to break free from this neo-colonial stranglehold, Nkrumah's CPP government embarked upon an ambitious programme of rapid industrialisation combined with agricultural expansion. The aim was twofold: firstly, to reduce the country's need for expensive imports by manufacturing for Ghana's own consumer needs, a policy known as import substitution; and secondly, not only to expand the range and scale of raw material exports, but to process many of them in Ghana and so earn more foreign exchange for the finished product. Thus Ghana would manufacture and export automobile tyres instead of raw latex, finished cloth instead of raw cotton, sawn timber instead of logs and aluminium instead of bauxite.

The emphasis of economic policy was upon rapid growth in order to sustain the government's ambitious programme of social, educational and health expenditure and it appeared that the only way to achieve this was through centralised, corporate socialism. The model of eastern Europe in those days seemed both clear and positive. Following this model, the CPP government intervened in every sector of the economy, setting up state-owned corporations to run gold mining, plantation agriculture, processing industries, transport and marketing. Huge investment was poured into the country's transport infrastructure and port facilities. New rail links were opened and trunk roads connected these to smaller villages. A national airline was established, Ghana Airways, and a national shipping line, the Black Star Line. The largest single investments were the Akosombo dam and hydro-electric project, one of the largest of its kind in the world, and the new port of Tema which was to service a nearby aluminium smelting plant.

The opening of the Akosombo hydro-electric plant in January 1966 was to be one of Nkrumah's last public functions as Head of State. It was said by later critics of Nkrumah that the main effect of Akosombo was to saddle Ghana with an enormous debt which the country could ill-afford. Even if accurate, however, this is a very short-term view and grossly underestimates the long-term significance of Akosombo. The hydro-electric project at Akosombo may not have catapulted Ghana into immediate industrial prosperity, as some contemporary propagandists had implied, but it did mark the beginning of Ghana's gradual industrial take-off. Without Akosombo little of the other infrastructural development would have been possible. Not only did Akosombo lay the foundations for the country's long-term development, it also enabled Ghana to weather the energy crisis of 1973 and, in due course, even to export electricity to her neighbours. It is only in the late 1980s and early 1990s, however, that the farsightedness of Nkrumah's investment programme is being fully realised and appreciated.

There is no doubt that Nkrumah's government achieved great infrastructural development, which made Ghana the envy of much of independent Africa. But at a cost! Ultimately, the social and political as well as economic costs were such that they undermined much of what had originally been achieved.

In basic economic terms the country was taken to the verge of bankruptcy. The £200 million reserve, accumulated in London during the colonial period, was rapidly turned into a huge deficit as Nkrumah's government committed itself to massive debts which the country could not sustain. At the same time development was distorted artificially away from the country's traditional economic base, peasant agriculture.

With the emphasis of investment centred on industry and infrastructure, agriculture, apart from the state plantations, failed to get the vital support it needed. Cocoa, the main export earner, and food production, both traditionally in the hands of private farmers, were left to fend for themselves. In fact the cocoa farmers suffered a positive disinvestment, since the state-owned Cocoa Marketing Board (CMB) followed the colonial practice of paying the cocoa farmers a low fixed rate for their produce, regardless of the world market price. Thus when the world cocoa market reached a record level of £450 a ton in the 1950s, the Ghanaian cocoa farmer received no more than £150 a ton. A net 'surplus' of £200 a ton went straight into government coffers for investment elsewhere. Although the CPP's investment programme ultimately benefited the nation countrywide, the issue of the cocoa price became a handy tool for whipping up political support for opponents of the CPP. It was thus no coincidence that so much of the opposition to Nkrumahist ideals was drawn from the cocoa farming regions of the country.

By the early 1960s population growth had outstripped the country's ability to feed itself and for the first time in her history Ghana became a net importer of food. At the same time cocoa prices on the world market were collapsing and, with no reserves to tide it over, the country experienced a severe shortage of foreign exchange. Basic consumer products disappeared from the shops of Accra and inflation soared to 30 per cent. An austerity budget was proposed in February 1966, but before it could be implemented, Nkrumah's government was overthrown.

Few were surprised when Nkrumah was overthrown.

His methods and his policies had provoked opposition from his earliest time in politics.

In the years before independence opposition to Nkrumah had coalesced around the National Liberation Movement (NLM). This had started as a disparate grouping of British-educated intellectuals and Asante aristocracy who saw no place for themselves alongside the 'verandah boys' of the CPP, but it soon gained the mass support of the cocoa farmers of Ashanti and the merchants and traders of Kumasi who distrusted the bureaucratic socialism that was emanating from Accra. The NLM was never a very constructive opposition in the parliamentary sense. They accused the CPP functionaries and ministers of corruption and abuse of power and they condemned the way the CPP had built a 'personality cult' around Nkrumah. More than that, however, they conducted their campaigns with violence in the streets of Kumasi, threatening to use force if necessary to overthrow the government itself. The assaults of the NLM's 'Action Troopers' on the CPP residents of Kumasi, in particular those of Fante New Town, was matched by equal retaliation from stalwarts of the CPP. In these violent clashes of the mid-1950s lay the seeds of a long-term ethnic enmity which was to stain the future of Ghanaian national life. It was not an auspicious start to parliamentary politics and the NLM's attitude and actions merely encouraged Nkrumah to disregard their criticisms as worthless.

Convinced that he was right in his social and economic policies, and with the opposition organising outside Parliament and on ethnic lines, Nkrumah became more and more intolerant and dictatorial. Soon after independence in 1957 he got Parliament to outlaw all political parties based upon 'tribal' or regional support. This forced the NLM and the Northern People's Party to disband. They merged to form the United Party (UP) under the leadership of Dr Kofi A. Busia, but they were never particularly 'united' and they were ineffective as a parliamentary opposition.

In 1958 the CPP pushed through the Preventive Detention Act, a blatant abuse of power which ultimately rebounded upon Nkrumah's reputation. Originally intended for use against suspected assassins and saboteurs, detention became a way of conveniently removing any opponents or critics of the CPP as Nkrumah became more and more paranoid about 'the enemy within'. Prominent and respected political figures such as J.B.Danquah and Obetsebi Lamptey were detained while Busia, leader of the parliamentary opposition, anticipated his own detention and fled into exile in 1959.

Even within the CPP itself Nkrumah grew increasingly intolerant of opposition. Following his election as first President of the First Republic in 1960, he took over the position of General Secretary of the CPP, in addition to his role as Life Chairman. Convinced that the country's increasing economic problems stemmed from the party's lack of commitment to his own view of socialism, Nkrumah purged the CPP of many of its senior members, including prominent figures such as K.A.Gbedemah and Kojo Botsio.

Left only with a rump of party sycophants, the personality cult of the Osagyefo ('The Leader', 'The Redeemer') now really took over and 'Nkrumahism' – socialism adapted to the African condition – was promoted as the only valid philosophy for the country. Nkrumah believed that he and the restructured CPP could now automatically be equated with the interests of the masses, but this was clearly not the case. As he was ruefully to recognise in exile, the CPP had never been a party of selfless socialists. By the end, Nkrumah's government had become a regime of self-serving bureaucrats and corrupt party hacks and its eventual overthrow was greeted with widespread relief.

The move to a one-party state in 1964 was possibly Nkrumah's greatest error of political judgement. From now on there was no constitutional way to change the government or even alter government policy without the physical removal of Nkrumah himself. There had already been at least three serious attempts upon Nkrumah's life. The first was a bomb attack in Accra back in 1955 in which nobody was seriously hurt. The second, a grenade attack in the northern village of Kulungugu in August 1962, killed a small boy and wounded Nkrumah in the back. It was never discovered who threw the grenade, but some weeks later three senior members of the CPP were put on trial for organising the attempt. When they were acquitted for lack of evidence, Nkrumah, convinced that they were guilty, dismissed the Chief Justice and had Parliament declare the acquittals null and void. In the weeks that followed the Kulungugu attack, supporters of the disbanded NLM showed their true colours. Carrying out a threat made in 1956, they went on the rampage in Accra, throwing grenades in the streets and killing up to thirty people. A prominent 'anti-communist' and former leader of the NLM, one of the 'Big Six' of 1948, Obetsebi Lamptey, was subsequently tried and convicted for supplying the grenades that were used in these attacks.

The third assassination attempt occurred in Accra in January 1964 just a few weeks before the referendum for the one-party state. A policeman fired a shot as Nkrumah was leaving Flagstaff House, but he missed his target and killed a bodyguard instead. Newspapers the next day reported that Nkrumah himself had wrestled his would-be assassin to the ground and disarmed him. Although they had the man who pulled the trigger, it was never discovered who was behind this third attempt. A large number of senior police officers were dismissed, creating enmity and distrust between Nkrumah and the police, and many known opponents of the government were detained, among them once again, J.B.Danquah.

Clearly Nkrumah's paranoia was not without foundation. However, in 1965, the death in detention of J.B. Danquah, regarded by many as the father of Ghanaian nationalism, became a potent symbol of how far the CPP had travelled from the nation's founding principles of freedom and justice for all.

In his last address to the National Assembly in February 1966, Nkrumah issued a prophetic warning:

> Let me emphasise that a one-party system of government ... must be an expression of the will of the masses working for the ultimate good and welfare of the people as a whole. [Otherwise it can] ... quickly develop into the most dangerous form of tyranny, despotism and oppression ...

Clearly Nkrumah had become so isolated from reality he had no idea that in many people's eyes his government had already reached that dangerous state of tyranny.

Opposition to Nkrumah and his socialist ideology was not confined to Ghana and Ghanaians. For most of his political life, Nkrumah had presented an audacious challenge to the interests of the 'West'. At a time of heightened Cold War rivalry between East and West, Nkrumah had played a leading role in steering emergent Africa on a course of non-alignment. In 1958 he had challenged French policy in Africa by helping Sékou Touré's Guinea to survive its independence. In 1961 he had accused the US Central Intelligence Agency (CIA) of complicity in the murder of Patrice Lumumba in the Congo. And he openly espoused the causes of the anti-imperialist 'freedom fighters' in the Portuguese colonies and in Rhodesia and South Africa.

Although most foreign investment in Ghana came from America and Western Europe, the capitalist West viewed the bilateral economic arrangements between Ghana and the socialist governments of Eastern Europe, the Soviet Union and China with the utmost suspicion and distrust. This was compounded in 1965 when Nkrumah published a book called *Neo-Colonialism: the last stage of imperialism* in which he exposed the exploitative machinations of capitalist multinational companies in Africa, especially those of the United States. He seemed surprised by the depth of the US government's hostility to the book.

By 1966 there were ten known CIA agents active in Accra. The US President, Lyndon Johnson, denied that the CIA 'threw the match into the haystack' of revolt, but he never denied that they provided the matches or stoked the fire. Certainly, the CIA were in regular contact with the plotters who were left in no doubt that the capitalist West would be pleased to see Nkrumah go.

The police and senior army officers who staged the coup of 1966 had their own specific reasons for acting as they did, not least of these being a recent cut-back in their budgets and a firm belief that Nkrumah was planning to commit the Ghanaian army to the liberation of Zimbabwe.

In the early hours of Thursday 24 February 1966, while the President was out of the country on a peace mission to Vietnam, the police and army seized control of Accra and announced on the radio that Nkrumah had been overthrown. With their action on that day, Ghana entered a new era of political instability.

There was dancing in the streets of Kumasi and Accra as people blamed their hardships on Nkrumah. Venting all their fears and frustrations on the symbols of Nkrumahism, they toppled his statue in the front of Parliament House. The state-owned press set the tone of hypocrisy with wild declarations such as: 'Tyranny is dead . . . democracy is reborn!' And it was not long before former 'loyal ministers' followed suit in a brazen orgy of self-effacement.

As so often happens with military *coups d'état*, the coup-makers protested their innocence and donned the garb of 'liberators'. In this instance, they formed a 'National Liberation Council' (NLC) of senior army and police officers, chaired by the recently-retired Lieutenant-General J.A. Ankrah. The NLC sought legitimacy by proving the extent of corruption in the previous regime. This was not very difficult, but the Commission of Enquiry was very selective about whom it investigated and a number of government and party functionaries were convicted on very flimsy evidence.

The British-trained officers of the NLC quickly laid out their right-wing credentials, making it clear that they were getting rid of socialism and 'returning Ghana to the Western fold'. Within weeks of the coup they had cancelled or suspended bilateral agreements with socialist countries, expelled all their technical personnel and closed down numerous worthy projects on the grounds that they were financed from the East. In doing so the NLC abandoned any serious attempt to break the country's neo-colonial dependence on the West. Thus the construction of the Tarkwa gold refinery was halted on the grounds that the refining of Ghana's gold could be done more cheaply abroad. Similarly, near Tema a series of cocoa storage silos were abandoned although near completion. With a potential capacity of 200 000 tons, these would have enabled Ghana to place up to half her annual cocoa crop in storage if the world market price was too low. But such an attitude was considered hostile to the interests of Western capitalism. When 350 Soviet crewmen working for the State Fishing Corporation were expelled from the country, ten of Ghana's deep-sea fishing trawlers were left to rust in Tema harbour. The shortfall in fish had to be made up by foreign frozen imports from 'Western' trawler fleets. Finally, although a number of state farms were sold off to private buyers, many were simply abandoned, their machinery left to rust and their crops to become overgrown with weeds.

The NLC turned with enthusiasm to the selling off of state corporations and many potentially profitable enterprises passed into foreign control. The financial rewards for turning away from socialism were soft loans from Britain, a temporary moratorium on loans from the United States and financial support from the IMF following a 30 per cent devaluation of the currency in July 1967. The benefits of devaluation were, however, lost to most Ghanaians for with cutbacks in investment and a decrease in the agricultural budget, production for export declined. Cocoa production, the mainstay of the economy, fell from 557 000 tons in 1965 to 334 000 tons in 1969. This was accompanied by cuts in public services, especially health and education, and rising unemployment as thousands of workers were laid off in the construction industry. By contrast, the defence budget was doubled and military salaries increased by more than 200 per cent.

The NLC period, 1966 – 69, can be summed up as little more than a sharing out of the spoils of power. Inflation was cut back slightly through a harsh wage freeze, but the budget deficit continued and with a deteriorating economic situation, the military were not anxious to stay in power any longer than necessary.

Soon after coming to power, the NLC had set up a Political Committee to supervise a return to civilian rule. The Committee was chaired by Dr K. Busia, who had recently returned from exile, and it was manned by a host of former failed politicians of the NLM and United Party. The intentions of the NLC were clear and the members of the Political Committee performed their task. They supervised the formation of a Constituent Assembly which devised a constitution to suit their own interests. One-party rule was specifically outlawed, the CPP was banned and most of the prominent CPP politicians were individually barred from standing for election for up to twelve years. Thus when the ban on party politics was lifted in 1969, Busia formed the 'Progress Party' (PP) out of remnants of the former United Party. With the direct backing of the military and the banning of the CPP, he had a clear advantage over any potential opponents.

In the General Election of September 1969 Busia's

Progress Party won 105 of the 140 seats in the Assembly, making a clean sweep of the Akan-speaking heartland of Brong-Ahafo, Ashanti and Central Regions. To the casual observer it may have appeared that, with the sole exception of Volta Region and Accra, a majority of Ghanaians had decided to trust the democratic credentials of 'Professor' K. Busia. There is little doubt, however, that in this election, the spectre of 'tribalism' had raised its ugly head once again in Ghanaian politics.

Although an element of anti-Nkrumahist rhetoric may have played a minor part in the outcome of the election, the most powerful determining factor was ethnic loyalty and prejudice. To be sure of outright victory, Busia had played the ethnic card by making an emotional appeal to the Akan-speaking peoples of the country, in particular, those of the powerful former kingdom of Ashanti. The Progress Party was widely seen to be the direct successor to the former United Party, which in turn had come from the NLM of the late 1950s. Only Komla Gbedemah's National Alliance of Liberals provided any opposition of note and most of their support was drawn from the Ewe of the Volta Region who clearly distrusted the Asante nationalism of the Progress Party. The feeling of distrust was mutual and merely reflected the animosity between Ewe and Asante which had already become apparent within the ruling NLC.

Despite the democratic rhetoric of the Progress Party and the high hopes of the electorate, the government of the Second Republic was a great disappointment. Busia proved no respecter of democracy, in fact, he became just as dictatorial as Nkrumah had ever been. He interfered with the independence of the judiciary. He sacked judges and fired newspaper editors when they disagreed with him. Moreover, there were strong rumours that the party was syphoning off gold to neighbouring Côte d'Ivoire to buy Peugeot cars for the party élite. Rumours such as this were probably prompted by the kind of close personal relationship which existed between Busia and Houphouët-Boigny who was known to have assisted the Progress Party in the past.

In his first year in office, Busia alienated many intellectuals when he sacked over 500 senior civil servants on the grounds that the constitution gave him the right to do so. Nearer the truth was the fact that many were suspected of having worked for the opposition during the election. Then, supposedly as a means of solving the unemployment problem, he introduced the Aliens Compliance Order which expelled from the country, without right of appeal, those not born in Ghana, apart from a few selected individuals such as foreign businessmen. Thus in the early months of 1970 over one million Africans were expelled to the neighbouring countries of Mali, Niger, Nigeria, Togo and Burkina Faso.

By the middle of 1971 the Busia government was facing mounting public criticism on a number of fronts. Six years of anti-socialist 'free market' policies had produced few tangible gains for the country as a whole. There was little long-term investment in agriculture. The proceeds of a boom cocoa harvest in 1970 were spent mostly on imports of luxury consumer goods to satisfy the urban bourgeoisie. There remained a balance of payments deficit, shortages of basic commodities in the shops, rising unemployment and huge foreign debts. Some of the opposition to Busia focused on his government's refusal to allow the ailing Nkrumah to return home to die. But this was merely symbolic of a wider sense of disillusionment.

Busia provoked further opposition by his attitude towards trades unionists and students. He crippled the Trades Union Congress (TUC) by banning the compulsory levying of dues on all union members; and he had a stormy relationship with the leadership of the National Union of Ghanaian Students (NUGS). On one occasion, in a fracas at the University of Science and Technology, a student leader was seen tugging at the shirt of the Prime Minister!

The intense antipathy between Busia and the NUGS leadership helped to prompt student support for the *coup d'état* of 1972. By then Busia had taken the provocative step of cutting the military budget and replacing certain military personnel with Progress Party sympathisers. Finally, in December 1971, with the economy in serious trouble, the government took the politically suicidal decision of devaluing the cedi by a drastic 48.6 per cent and imposing a 5 per cent 'national development' levy. The immediate result was an increase in the price of imports, and a further rise in inflation.

Intervention by the military was not an obvious solution, but it had been done before and people were not at all surprised when it happened again. Thus the bloodless coup staged by Colonel Ignatius Kutu Acheampong on 13 January 1972 was accepted by Ghanaians with a certain sense of inevitability. The parallels with 1966 were plain for all to see and Acheampong himself based his justification upon the precedent of 1966.

In February 1966 the *Daily Graphic* had cited rising inflation, unemployment and shortages of consumer goods as the main grievances of the people which had justified the country's first *coup d'état*. Its widespread acceptance legitimised the principle of military intervention whenever the economy could be said to be in a similar 'chaotic condition'. Acheampong ensured that the 1966 coup had not been a single, never-to-be-repeated action. His intervention in 1972 established the military takeover as a part of the Ghanaian political process. This concept was strengthened by the fact that Acheampong and his co-conspirators initially paraded as erstwhile Nkrumahists who sought to reverse the 'neo-colonialist sell-out' of the Busia administration and return Ghana to some of the best of the self-respecting principles of Nkrumah's day.

Citing corruption and mismanagement as the principal reasons for the coup, Acheampong was careful to disassociate himself from the dark side of Nkrumah's government. Nevertheless, he was able to revive the people's sympathy for Nkrumah's socialist ideals when on the death of the Osagyefo in exile in April 1972, he ordered the return of his body to Ghana and awarded him a full state funeral in Accra.

Before this, however, Acheampong's National Redemption Council (NRC) had won immediate popular support by reversing the fiscal policies of the previous regime. He cancelled the 5 per cent development levy, revalued the cedi and then, setting up a popular cry of *'Yentua, yentua'* ('We won't pay, we won't pay'), he repudiated many of the country's foreign debts. This may have won Acheampong popular support in the short term, but it was guaranteed to make the economic situation worse in the long run.

Freed temporarily from the stranglehold of foreign debt, Acheampong declared his aim to be economic self-reliance, stressing that this would only be achieved through austerity and hard work.

The main focus of Acheampong's early years was Operation Feed Yourself (OFY). This involved a huge drive to achieve self-sufficiency in the country's two principal food crops, rice and maize. OFY was widely welcomed in both town and countryside and it ushered in a brief period of boom in food production. Although admirable and imaginative, the success of OFY was short-lived. Enthusiasm alone would not grow food. The oil crisis of 1973 affected the importation of vital inputs, and the attempt to switch to mechanisation was poorly planned and implemented. By 1975 these and other factors had crippled the initiative and it became clear to all that OFY had run its course.

By 1975 the Ghanaian economy was moving into deep recession and Acheampong clearly did not know what to do about it. On top of the oil price rises of 1973, came drought and falling cocoa production. No attention had been paid to investment in the country's infrastructure since 1966. As a result, roads began to fall apart and industrial and farm machinery packed up for lack of spares.

Until this time the NRC had been made up largely of those middle-ranking officers who had staged the original coup of 1972. Its exclusion of the service commanders had always posed a problem of protocol within the military hierarchy. Faced with an emerging economic crisis in 1975 the service commanders, fearing that the military as a whole would be discredited, seized the initiative and forced through a change in the structure of the NRC which almost ousted Acheampong himself. The 'Supreme Military Council' (SMC) which replaced the NRC contained the commanders of all the military services as well as the Inspector General of Police. Acheampong retained sole responsibility for finance and defence, but he clearly lacked the ability to solve the country's problems. Policy-making entered the realms of farce when the Head of State launched an essay competition for suggestions on how to improve the economy! He topped this in June 1977 by launching a national week of prayer. The only thing that Acheampong could think of doing himself, when faced with a rising budget deficit, was to print more money. This simply fuelled inflation which had soared to more than 100 per cent by 1976.

Combined with declining national production and an excess of money in the economy, the cedi became more and more overvalued in terms of foreign exchange. World cocoa prices soared to record levels in 1977, but all the gain was syphoned off by the government or corrupt individuals. Cocoa farmers and others found it was simply not worth their while producing for the export market. Many farmers abandoned export crops in favour of growing food for themselves while others smuggled cocoa across the border to Côte d'Ivoire where more realistic prices could be obtained. Meanwhile, with falling industrial and commercial food production, demand for imports rose and Acheampong's government found itself turning once again to foreign money-lenders for support. By 1977 it had run up debts as large as any of its predecessors. The incompetence and mismanagement of the early years was coming home to roost and it was soon clear that the government had lost control of the economy.

As the economy fell apart, those military officers in positions of power began to help themselves to the country's dwindling coffers. Senior military officers, now in charge of ministries and state corporations, used their positions to look after their own interests. The scope for their nefarious activities was almost infinite. It ranged from diverting state funds and selling import licences, to using army labour and equipment to build private houses for themselves. At the same time those military officers who headed state corporations left themselves open to exploitation by corrupt civilian businessmen who manipulated contracts and deals to make illegal fortunes for themselves.

The Acheampong government, widely recognised as disastrous for the country, is most vividly remembered for its institution of corruption on a massive scale and for the UNIGOV experiment. The former hastened Ghana's dramatic economic decline. The latter provided the opportunity for the downfall of the SMC regime.

In the name of exercising some control over the distribution of scarce consumer commodities, the SMC instituted a system of paper 'chits' for the release of goods from state-owned factories and warehouses. Known popularly as *kalabule,* the chit system became the basis for an all-embracing habit of corruption which permeated every level of society, beginning with the government bureaucrat who issued the original chit and ending with the man or woman in the street who bought the actual goods at grossly inflated prices. In between lay a shady assortment of middlemen who made an unproductive and parasitic living out of buying and selling chits for profit. *Kalabule* was the curse of the

Acheampong years and the term came to be used for any kind of corruption or profiteering, including the selling of any goods above the official controlled prices, which hardly anybody observed. With rampant inflation and fast eroding salaries, almost everyone was up to some kind of fiddle as the only way to survive. Moral righteousness was a rare commodity.

Those who could not stand it any longer sought help through emigration. While some went to Côte d'Ivoire to work on the plantations, many more trekked to Nigeria which was benefiting from the boom in oil prices. Others who could afford it or who had the connections went to Western Europe, often via scholarships to the Soviet Union or Eastern Europe. This was the era of the 'Hamburgers', those who joined the Ghanaian network in Western Germany and, working in all kinds of clandestine employment, managed to accumulate funds and send home goods for selling in Accra. The Acheampong years witnessed a great Ghanaian diaspora of the country's academics and professionals who sought worthwhile employment in other African countries or in the developed world of Europe and North America.

Realising that he needed to regain some kind of legitimacy for his ailing government, but unwilling to release the reins of power, Acheampong sought to devise a new constitution which would guarantee a permanent place for himself and the military in the government of the country. In the closing months of 1976 the SMC began to float its scheme for a new constitution. It was to be known as 'Union Government' or UNIGOV.

The SMC proposal was for a non-party government with direct military and police participation enshrined in the constitution. Acheampong seems to have believed that this gesture towards civilian representation would satisfy his critics. In January 1977 he set up an *ad hoc* Committee to sound out opinion and draw up specific proposals for the UNIGOV concept. But the very idea of seeking opinion provided his opponents with a rallying call for their discontent. NUGS and the general student body were the most vocal critics of the scheme. In May 1977 they staged simultaneous demonstrations at all three universities, demanding the immediate resignation of Acheampong. In violent clashes with the military, one student was killed and the campaign had its first martyr. The universities were closed, re-opened briefly in June and promptly closed again when the students went on strike. The Association of Recognised Professional Bodies, representing lawyers, doctors, university teachers and others, came out in June with denunciation of the SMC and called for its resignation, a call echoed by the Christian Council.

In a dawn broadcast on 1 July 1977 Acheampong rejected these demands and his reaction provoked a general strike by members of the Association of Recognised Professional Bodies. By the middle of July, with the country grinding to a halt and revolution in the air, Acheampong had been forced to concede that he would hand over to a civilian government by 1 July 1979. He still did not give up on the UNIGOV concept but he promised to put it to a referendum to be held on 30 March 1978.

The SMC conducted its campaign for the UNIGOV referendum in a way that made it clear that its senior military officers were determined to play a role in any future government of the country. Their attitude and actions ensured that the referendum would become a vote of confidence on the record of Acheampong and his government.

Defying the ban on party politics, the opposition organised itself into a series of political fronts. The largest and most prominent was the People's Movement for Freedom and Justice (PMFJ), formed in January 1978. Among its leaders were General A.A.Afrifa, final chairman of the NLC in 1969 and head of the transitional presidential council in the first year of Busia's government, William of the 'Big Six' of 1948, and Komla Gbedemah, former prominent member of the CPP and later leader of the parliamentary opposition in the Second Republic.

Meanwhile, Dr Kwame Safo-Adu, Minister of Agriculture under Busia, Victor Owusu and some members of the Progress Party formed the Front for the Prevention of Dictatorship. Other former politicians who were prominent in the anti-UNIGOV campaign included Dr J.K. Bilson, who later founded the Third Force, and G.W.Amartefio, who became known as 'Mr No' for the outspoken manner of his opposition to UNIGOV.

The campaign in favour of Acheampong's proposals was not confined to the military alone. Civilian support was to be found in the Organisers' Council, the Friends, the Patriots, the African Youth Command and numerous other *ad hoc* organisations. This motley crowd of UNIGOV supporters contained many personalities that were clearly identified with the former CPP, reflecting to some extent Acheampong's early leanings towards the Nkrumahist tradition. Several of these individuals were later active in the founding of the People's National Party (PNP) in 1979. Thus within the various campaign movements, both pro- and anti-UNIGOV, lay the makings of Ghana's traditional party alignments in the anticipated 'Third Republic'.

Campaigning was vociferous and effective and by referendum day on 30 March, it was clear that UNIGOV would never win majority support. This prompted Acheampong to intervene in a way which ultimately brought about his downfall. The official regulations for the referendum stated that counting of votes would take place at individual polling stations, as soon as voting was completed. But on polling day itself the SMC issued a directive on the radio ordering that the polling boxes were to be collected up and taken to regional centres for counting. The Electoral Commissioner, Justice I.K. Abban bravely challenged this in writing, denouncing it as illegal. He was promptly sacked and, as orders went out for his arrest, he went into hiding, having published the first two results just before midnight. They showed a clear defeat for UNIGOV. When, the next day, the state-owned press announced that UNIGOV had been approved by 54 per cent to 46 per cent, nobody seriously believed it, especially since the announcement was accompanied by widespread arrests and the banning of all opposition groups.

Strikes persisted throughout the country and by June it was clear that the SMC was doomed. The mass of Ghanaian people had become highly politicised during the campaign for the referendum and some kind of violent revolt seemed likely if the SMC was not removed.

On 5 July 1978, with several simultaneous plots hatching among the military, a small group of officers isolated Acheampong from his bodyguard and forced him to sign his own resignation.

Lieutenant-General Fred Akuffo took over the chairmanship of the SMC and announced on the radio that Acheampong had been asked to resign because he had been running 'a one-man show' and had not been heeding the advice of the Supreme Military Council. Although a few senior officers were dismissed and some civilians were brought into government, Akuffo made it clear that the new SMC – popularly known as SMC II – was simply a reformed version of the same military government. No legal action was taken against any of those dismissed for corruption or mismanagement and it appeared to many that the palace coup of 5 July had been little more than an attempt by certain military officers to stave off open revolt and to distance themselves from the worst abuses of the Acheampong government. These suspicions were confirmed when Akuffo announced that he would stick with the UNIGOV concept in his preparation of a new constitution for the return to civilian rule in 1979.

Akuffo attempted to win popular support for his

'government of transition' by releasing all those who had been detained in the wake of the March referendum and by appealing to political exiles to return from abroad. But he could not win support for the UNIGOV idea and his government came under continuing attack from the same people who had opposed Acheampong – students, professionals and Church leaders. The civilian population sensed that the military had been discredited and that they had them on the run. There were widespread strikes in almost every sector of the economy and even the civil servants went on strike for three days in November. After initially declaring a 'State of Emergency', the SMC realised it would have to capitulate to civilian political pressure. In December 1978 Akuffo announced the setting up of a Constituent Assembly to draw up a constitution and, abandoning all hope of imposing UNIGOV, he lifted the ban on political parties on 1 January 1979.

With the inclusion of civilians in the government of 1978, a sincere attempt was made by Akuffo to arrest the economic decline within the country. The first and most important decision was to devalue the currency. This was very badly needed, especially after Acheampong's revaluation of 1972. The subsequent decline in the economy and the accompanying excess printing of currency notes had rendered the Ghanaian cedi almost valueless. On the parallel market the cedi was worth a fraction of the official exchange rate. For years foreign currency had been bought at the official rate through special import licences and promptly exchanged on the parallel market for many times that amount. It had been simply another outlet for corrupt friends of the government.

In September 1978 the cedi was put on a floating scale and by March 1979 it had been devalued by 58 per cent. The whole concept of devaluation, however, attracted the wrath of the radical left, especially the student leadership which regarded it as a sell-out to the forces of imperialism.

This was a political platform which had gained credence in the 1971–72 period because of the close association of Busia's government with the financiers of the capitalist West. Acheampong's reversal of Busia's devaluation was viewed by the left as a victory for socialist ideology. Henceforth devaluation as a concept entered the socialist rhetoric of the Ghanaian left as a symbol of a sell-out to the imperialist West. It was a stance of dubious value which was to return to haunt the Ghanaian body politic in the 1980s.

The other major economic decision taken by Akuffo's government was the changing of the country's currency notes. Between 10 and 26 March all the old currency notes, popularly known as 'Acheampong's cedis' were withdrawn and new cedi notes were issued in their place. Currency in bank accounts was exchanged on a one to one basis, but notes in circulation were penalised. Sums of up to ₵5000 were exchanged at the rate of ten old for seven new, while for sums over ₵5000 the exchange rate fell to ten old for five new. Illegal hoards of money kept abroad were struck out altogether.

In the circumstances of the institutionalised corruption which characterised the SMC regimes, the currency exchange was an exercise which, no matter how worthy in intent, was open to widespread abuse. Some senior army officers were seen to have been hurriedly buying cars and property in the few days before the change-over was announced, and there was ample scope for exploitation during the exchange itself. As ever, those who suffered most were the rural poor who could not get to banks in time and lost much of their cash savings to unscrupulous *kalabule* dealers who bought and sold currency notes as if there was no tomorrow. Businessmen and bankers, with their bank accounts exchanged at par, had little to lose and much to gain from the deal: a point that aroused considerable antipathy towards the Lebanese business community. To the long-oppressed and exploited majority the whole exercise seemed like an attempt by a corrupt and discredited military government and its business friends to go on one final orgy of self-enrichment at the expense of the masses. It is an attitude to be borne in mind when considering the mass support for the June 4th Revolution when it came.

In straight economic terms, the immediate effect of the cedi exchange was to reduce drastically the amount of money in circulation and this in turn had a welcome impact upon the rate of inflation. The consequences of fifteen years of economic neglect, however, had taken their toll and the Akuffo government did not have the time, the popular mandate, or even the inclination, to steer the economy in any new direction. Theirs was simply a holding operation. Unfortunately, it did not appear that the newly emergent political parties were likely to fare much better.

Immediately the ban on party politics had been lifted in January 1979, the old party machinery had swung into action. There were new names to the parties, but much of the old division between CPP and UP/PP tendencies remained. The Nkrumahist inheritance was taken up by the People's National Party (PNP), formed by many of the 'old guard' CPP members who had fallen out with Nkrumah in the 1960s. They had access to the old CPP networks, although they had lost much of their socialist credentials over the years. The 'purer' socialist inheritance was taken up by Johnny Hansen who formed the People's Revolutionary Party (PRP). This, in fact, was later to merge with the PNP. Opposing them, the Popular Front Party (PFP), headed by Victor Owusu, represented the Busia tendency of the former Progress Party. In between the two traditional divisions lay a multitude of parties and personal interest groups.

The parties began campaigning even before the constitution was devised. They were mostly pretty vague about economic policy and the principal parties drew much of their rhetoric and their rationale from the party politics of the two previous republics. All promised great tomorrows, with very little substance or analysis of the country's real economic crisis.

The Constituent Assembly sat from January to March 1979 and came up with a draft constitution which favoured an American-style Executive Presidency and a 140-member National Assembly. The draft was sent to General Akuffo for SMC approval. By early May the Constituent Assembly was still waiting for the SMC's reaction. It remained unclear just exactly who was to promulgate the constitution, the Constituent Assembly or the Head of State. There were rumours and suspicions in some circles that perhaps the SMC was deliberately delaying the promulgation and was having second thoughts about the handover. On the surface, however, there was no obvious foundation for these suspicions. During May the tempo of campaigning built up and, on the bland assumption that all was well, the parties went into top gear for the general and presidential elections, scheduled for 18 June.

Despite the pre-election fever, there was a certain sense of unreality in the air. Things were going a little too smoothly. A long era of oppressive and disastrous military rule was coming to an end. Were the military *really* going to hand over power? Was anybody going to be called to account for the past seven years and more of mismanagement and corruption which had dragged the Ghanaian economy to such appalling depths? There were a lot of old scores to be settled and the *kalabule* system was still as rife as ever in all walks of life. Were the new politicians *really* going to be any better than the previous regimes?

Political instability had a long history in Ghana and while enthusiastic party political leaders lived in their 'Fool's Paradise' of pre-election promises, some more thoughtful or more cynical members of the electorate had their doubts. No one, however, imagined for a moment that the Ghanaian body politic was about to receive the rudest shock in its twenty-two years of independent history.

Chapter 2

Rawlings and the June 4th Revolution

Tuesday 15 May 1979 dawned much like any other over the city of Accra. The rains were late that year and clear skies showed promise of another hot day. People made their way to work on foot, by 'tro-tro' truck, by taxi or by private car, unaware of the events that had been happening under cover of darkness the previous night. The women of Makola market were setting up their stalls and ministries and offices were opening for work. Suddenly the normal scenes of cheerful bustle were thrown into panic by that most potent of weapons in modern Ghana – rumour.

It started soon after 8.30 a.m. with the sound of gunfire from the direction of Burma Camp on the north-east side of the city. Within minutes rumour had spread the news to the centre of town, multiplying the cause with every mile, from 'The students are fighting the police' or 'The army and police are fighting each other', to 'The soldiers are marching on the city, shooting everyone in sight'! In the centre of town nobody waited to confirm the rumours. Panic reigned as stalls were abandoned in Makola market. The streets and major roads into the city were quickly jammed with traffic as drivers tried to turn their cars and their passengers simply got out and ran. Everywhere people were fleeing in the direction of Kaneshie and McCarthy Hill, away from the city centre and away from Burma Camp.

It was several hours before people realised that there was no real danger and life returned to normal. However, the ease with which people believed the rumours and the depth of popular panic were indicative of a widespread lack of trust. It reflected the collective sense of unreality about the apparent ease of the current moves towards civilian rule.

Later in the day it was announced from Burma Camp that an attempted rising by some Air Force officers had indeed taken place, but that the perpetrators had been captured and they would soon be put on trial. The next morning the state-owned *Daily Graphic* probably reflected the general civilian feeling at the time when it described the 'disturbance' as 'totally unwarranted and completely out of place'. In the opinion of the *Graphic*, Ghanaians had had enough of the 'constant oscillation' between military and civilian rule and it could not understand any possible justification for another coup at this critical moment in the country's history. It concluded that the would-be coup-makers must have been acting from a purely selfish desire to extend the duration of military rule beyond the scheduled date of 1 July.

On the afternoon of Wednesday 16 May the military authorities in Burma Camp named the leader of the uprising as Flight Lieutenant J. J. Rawlings of Air Force Station, Accra. Ghanaians generally, however, were still none the wiser as to the reason for the mutiny. Rawlings himself was little-known outside the military establishment. Most people knew nothing of his origins and, until the revelations of the promised Military Tribunal, they knew even less about his possible motivation.

Jerry Rawlings John was born in Accra of a Ghanaian mother and Scottish father on 22 June 1947. Although he was initially baptised by the Bremen Mission, he was later re-baptised a Roman Catholic. His name became Jerry John Rawlings when he enlisted in the Air Force in 1967. The birth of the child placed Jerry's father in an awkward situation for he was already married to a British woman and this made it impossible for him to acknowledge his son.

If it had come to the notice of the colonial authorities that he had had a child by a Ghanaian woman, he would have been sent back to Britain in disgrace. He was saved from his dilemma by Victoria Agbotui, the mother of Jerry John who, out of compassion for the man, agreed not to do anything that would aggravate the situation.

Jerry was therefore brought up entirely by his mother, a strict and strong-minded woman who did not hesitate to beat her children in order to instill in them her own strong moral code of honesty, integrity and personal discipline. She struggled to raise enough money to put him through private schooling, sending him in due course to the prestigious Achimota secondary school.

Jerry John was well-known and generally well-liked at school, both for his strong and fun-loving personality and for his striking good looks. Although he was teased at times by his black Ghanaian peers for being a 'rusty white man', he was well able to stand up for himself and also stood up for other children. Contemporaries recall that his qualities of leadership showed from an early age. He would not tolerate bullying and he readily came to the defence of any 'underdog' who might be being mistreated by his or her classmates.

The young Jerry had developed a fascination for flying from a very early age. He vividly remembers receiving a sharp smack upon his back from his mother when at the age of six he told her he wanted to be a pilot. His mother was determined that he should go to university and enter that most respected of professions, medicine. But Jerry was never one for hours of academic study. He preferred the active life and his mother was bitterly disappointed when he left school after 'O' levels and moved out of the family home.

For a year the young man was undecided about his future and he admits that he led a pretty wild life, picking up odd jobs here and there, while all the time searching for a more purposeful existence that would suit his particular talents. As a schoolboy in his mid-teens in the early 1960s, Jerry, like his contemporaries, had been well aware of the corruption of Nkrumah's final years. During the school holidays he had worked on construction sites for the resettlement of people relocated from their villages by the building of the Akosombo dam. He had seen the weak and crumbling walls of the houses they were building, caused by the syphoning off of cement for sale on the private market. He had been brought up to believe that people in authority should display the highest standards of integrity and yet everywhere he saw numerous examples of people in authority illegally enriching themselves at the expense of the poor and the helpless. The decaying walls of the people's houses were merely symbolic of a deeper moral corruption which greatly disturbed the highly moralistic youth.

In his last year at school, the coup of 1966 had brought the military to power with a strong commitment to abolish the corruption of the previous regime. As yet unsullied by the corrupting influence of political power, the military still had a reputation for honour, discipline and integrity. It was this reputation, combined with his own unquenched desire to fly, which made the young man decide to join the Air Force.

In August 1967, at the age of twenty, Jerry John signed up as a Flight Cadet at Takoradi Air Force Station. When signing on he wrote out his name in full, Jerry Rawlings John, but the Air Force administration, assuming John to be a second Christian name, recorded Rawlings as his surname. He was indifferent to the change and has thus been known ever since as Jerry John Rawlings.

One hundred and twenty cadets signed up with him for the aptitude test. Flight Cadet Rawlings made it through the aptitude test and went on to train as a pilot. Senior officers noted that Rawlings displayed a natural talent for flying. He seemed to love every moment of it, the excitement, the concentration and the challenge. He won the

'Speedbird Trophy' for best pilot in 1969, beating some who were a set ahead of him in training. Rawlings was commissioned as a Pilot Officer in 1969, was promoted to Flight Officer in 1971 and became a Flight Lieutenant in 1978.

During his early years as a flying officer, Rawlings continued his long-term friendship with the woman who was to become his wife, Nana Konadu Agyeman. They had been close friends since their time at Achimota school together. She had stayed on at Achimota to do her 'A' levels before going to university and becoming a graphic designer. Although Rawlings had had many relationships with other women in the meantime, he recalls that he had always held Nana Konadu in specially high esteem and it seemed to him inevitable that they should marry one day. By 1976 that day had still not arrived and Nana Konadu went to work in Switzerland. Soon after her return from Switzerland, however, the couple became engaged and they married in January 1977.

Married life for Rawlings did not mean settling down to quiet domesticity. In fact he was just about to enter upon the most turbulent period of his career.

If he had hoped to find high moral integrity and a personal sense of purpose in the military life, Rawlings was quickly disillusioned, even before he had finished his formal training. After three years in government, the military had revealed itself as susceptible to corruption as any other sector of society. Rawlings observed with mounting anger the corruption of the Acheampong years and the contempt with which the senior officers of the military treated the rank and file. The country was spiralling into poverty while senior officers and friends of Acheampong were getting rich at the expense of the poor and the weak.

Throughout 1976 and 1977 the Air Force, like everything else in the country, was being rapidly run down through gross neglect. The ranks did not get enough food to eat, their wages were eroded by inflation and for someone like

Rawlings there was additional frustration because there was not even any regular flying practice, through lack of fuel and spare parts to service the aircraft.

His Group Captain, Frank Okyne, recalls that Rawlings was never one to take things easy and so he put him in charge of the Air Force boxing team. This brought Rawlings into close and regular contact with the other ranks for whom he had always felt a greater empathy than for the officer corps. He was, in addition, a keen horseman so he was often at the Recce riding stables which gave him regular access to the men of Recce Regiment with whom he became a popular figure. Simple physical activity on its own, however, seemed never to be enough to satisfy the man.

Rawlings had developed a strong moral awareness and he was constantly searching for philosophical as well as practical answers to the questions which life posed. On the intellectual front, Richard Bach's *Jonathan Livingstone Seagull,* which he read around this time, articulated very well Rawlings' views on perfection and the quest for freedom. He was fascinated by the conflict between selfishness and selflessness which he found in Ian Rand's *Fountain Head* and a book called *Rebel Priest* also struck a chord with him. In his early adult life Rawlings had considered entering the priesthood as a means to work for social justice, but he soon realised that he did not have the temperament for the priestly life. Nevertheless, Rawlings retained a consuming passion to solve the country's problems.

By 1977 he was considering leaving the Air Force altogether and joining the police. A policeman to Rawlings was a symbol of law and order, a symbol of justice, and for a while he thought that by joining the police force he would be able to clear up much of the corruption and injustice in society. It is typical of the contradictions in the man, however, that at about the same time as he was considering a career as a policeman, he was also contemplating armed robbery as a means of re-balancing the economic disparity which he saw all around him. He even assembled a team of soldiers of high integrity and self-discipline to carry out the deeds. They believed in the moral justification of what Rawlings described as 'taking money back from the constitutionally protected thieves' and giving it to the poor and the exploited. Intended mainly as a symbolic gesture, to generate an atmosphere of defiance in the people, the armed robbery scheme was abandoned because the soldiers he had chosen refused to work alongside one of their colleagues who had known criminal tendencies.

Thus, in the long term, practicalities intervened and Rawlings remained within the Air Force. There is little doubt that he had a great respect for the spirit and the code of honour of the military life and yet he saw it daily being betrayed by the most senior officers in the forces. Bearing in mind his temperament and his desire for action to right injustice, it was inevitable that Rawlings, like many other middle-ranking officers of the time, should become involved in plotting the overthrow of Acheampong. One of his most audacious schemes entailed the bombing of Acheampong's room in Burma Camp in Accra. His search for a suitable landing site in the vicinity of the capital took him to the plains beyond the university and it was while visiting Legon that he first made contact with some of the radical student critics of the government.

Early in 1978, soon after the UNIGOV referendum, Group Captain Okyne assembled a durbar which was an opportunity for the squadron's young officers and other ranks to express their anger and frustration. Rawlings was said to have been the most out-spoken at the meeting. He demanded the immediate removal of Acheampong and cited General Joshua Hamidu and Okyne who seemed to him at that time to be the sort of clean and honest officers who could take over the country and clear it of corruption.

According to Captain Boakye Djan, an officer in Military Intelligence, Rawlings' coup-making potential had been a cause of concern to certain senior officers for some considerable time. Military Intelligence already had a file on him and he was periodically brought in for questioning. General Akuffo and Air Commodore Boakye, both members of the SMC, appear to have been anxious that Rawlings might act before they themselves had a chance to move against Acheampong; and it was clear that the young man was more likely to lead a revolution of the lower ranks than the sort of cosy palace coup which Akuffo had in mind. According to Group Captain Okyne, Rawlings was called before Air Commodore Boakye in the presence of Okyne and warned to stop his clandestine activities. Rawlings had always felt a certain admiration for Commodore Boakye and he regretted the Commodore's close association with Acheampong. The young Flight Lieutenant therefore boldly demanded of the Commander of the Air Force, 'Why don't you resign from the SMC?'

It is indicative of the depths to which the upper echelons of the military had sunk that instead of reprimanding Rawlings for insubordination, Boakye went on the defensive and sought to justify himself and his position. His protestations of good intent earned him no respect from the angry young Flight Lieutenant.

Rawlings' initial expectations of the Akuffo palace coup of July 1978 were soon disillusioned and he came to regard the whole affair as a useless waste of time. Nothing of significance had been changed and the frustration and resentment of the lower ranks continued to simmer below the surface.

In what was probably an attempt to remove a potential trouble-maker at a time of crisis for Akuffo's government, Rawlings was sent on a training course to Pakistan towards the end of 1978. Strikes were widespread in Ghana at the time and Akuffo had recently declared a State of Emergency.

According to Rawlings' own recollection, he felt certain that an uprising was imminent and he was reluctant to leave the country at such a critical time. He went as he was ordered, but soon after arriving at Peshawar training school in northern Pakistan, he requested leave to return home, pleading problems in the country and anxiety for his wife and six-month-old child. By the time he returned to Ghana in January 1979, Akuffo had temporarily defused the situation by ending the State of Emergency, lifting the ban on party politics and establishing a Constituent Assembly to draw up a new constitution.

For Rawlings, however, this was not enough. Those who had disgraced their military uniforms and brought the country to its knees must be called to account. So far Acheampong himself had merely been retired from the army and placed in custody. No action had been brought against him or any others of the former SMC. It appeared to Rawlings that if the military was ever to regain its self-respect in a future civilian administration, it must purge itself of corruption at the highest level. Yet there was no sign that this was going to happen. The relationship between the SMC and the budding politicians of the future 'Third Republic' was just a little too cosy. In Rawlings' view, if something drastic were not done in these last few months of military rule, the corruption and injustices of the past seven years would merely be perpetuated in a different guise. At the same time he was acutely aware of the anger and the mutiny that were boiling within the ranks. He knew the hatred that they felt for many of their senior officers and he feared for the consequences if some action were not taken soon.

On 1 May 1979 the SMC announced that Acheampong was being stripped of his military rank, deprived of his retirement benefits, released from custody and confined to his home village in Ashanti Region. Despite clear evidence of corruption and abuse of power, he was not being put on public trial. Two days later it was revealed by a committee investigating malpractices that Major-Generals E. K. Utuka and R. E. A. Kotei, both former members of the SMC, had been found guilty of embezzling huge quantities of money from impounded timber in 1977. No court prosecution was proposed for them either.

These two incidents appear to have been the final straw for Rawlings. Fearing that the lower ranks might lose the will to fight, given the capability of the ruling group to manipulate events, Rawlings decided it was time to make his move.

Rawlings has spoken on numerous occasions about his motivation and actions on the night of 14-15 May 1979, so that his own version of events has gained a certain orthodoxy. The following account is drawn from a combination of the evidence at the subsequent trial, Rawlings' contemporary public statements and private interviews for this book.

The primary purpose of Rawlings' mutiny on the night of 14 – 15 May seems to have been, as he claimed, to force a dialogue with the senior military command. He drew his co-conspirators from the lower ranks of the Air Force and the Army although he did not explain to them the limited nature of his intended action. During the early part of the night Rawlings and his men broke into the Air Force ammunition dump and seized enough weapons and ammunition to arm themselves. They then retired to the bush to wait.

Rawlings had originally intended to make his move at midnight but, as he recollects it, sensing the vengeful anger of the men under his command, he decided to postpone the action for several hours. He feared that if he made his move too early, the darkness would give his men the sort of courage that they needed to spark off a terrible slaughter of officers which he, on his own, would be powerless to stop.

At 2.00 a.m., with dawn only a few hours away, Rawlings decided it was safe to make his move. He returned with his men to Air Force Station, seized a couple of vehicles and arrested the duty officer, Flight Lieutenant Joe Atiemo. They then proceeded to Recce Headquarters where Rawlings positioned his men in front of the gates of the Recce armoured garage. The idea was to separate the regiment from its arms and ammunition. During the course of the operation they arrested a total of ten Air Force and Army officers and held them hostage. With the coming of the dawn, as Rawlings had anticipated, the courage that comes with darkness waned and his small band of followers dwindled to little more than half a dozen.

Sometime after dawn Rawlings sent a man to set off the alarm and the Recce Commanding Officer, Major Suleimana, soon arrived upon the scene. Quickly sizing up the situation, Suleimana rushed to the Recce Magazine where he obtained enough armoured cars and ammunition to quell the mutiny. Shots were exchanged, an Air Force officer was killed and Rawlings agreed to disarm his men and give himself up.

With the benefit of hindsight a number of people have suggested that Akuffo's biggest mistake was to put Rawlings and his men on public trial. But Akuffo, apparently unaware of the mutinous feelings in the ranks, had no particular reason to do otherwise. There had been a long tradition in Acheampong's time of putting attempted coup-makers on public trial. With a general election barely a month away, Akuffo had every reason to believe that he had the credibility of the civilian population and that the remaining weeks of his regime were quite secure.

It was thus with an air of self-satisfaction that the SMC ordered Major-General Odartey Wellington to award medals for bravery to twelve officers and twenty-three other ranks for their part in quelling the uprising of 'a few misguided individuals'. This was crowned the following week by an official visit from the widely-respected Nigerian Head of State, General Obasanjo. Referring to the Ghanaian Head of State as 'my brother and colleague General Akuffo', Obasanjo congratulated the SMC on its integrity and its orderly move towards civilian rule. That weekend, with the praise of General Obasanjo still ringing in his ears, a supremely self-confident General Akuffo set off for Senegal on his final diplomatic mission abroad, a two-day Heads of Government meeting of the Economic Community of West African States (ECOWAS). The head of the SMC was thus absent from the country when Rawlings and his six co-conspirators were first brought before the Military Tribunal in Burma Camp on Monday 28 May.

Nana Konadu Rawlings had been denied access to her husband during his two-week imprisonment and had found that a number of people whom she had assumed to be her friends now sought to distance themselves from her. However, she managed to acquire the legal services of the President of the Council of the Bar Association, W. Adumoah Bossman, and the widely-respected lawyer and intellectual, Tsatsu Tsikata, to defend her husband at his trial.

By the time Rawlings and his co-defendants were admitted to the special court, the hall was packed by soldiers and airmen from the lower ranks. Journalists were also admitted to the court and their verbatim reporting of the proceedings played a vital role in promoting the revolution that was soon to follow. The first day's hearing was taken up by the opening address from the Director of Public Prosecutions, Mr G.E.K. Aikins. In presenting his summary of evidence, Mr Aikins read from the statement of the accused as well as from the evidence of the officers who had been taken hostage and to whom Rawlings had explained his motivation. Deprived of his public forum on 15 May by the prompt action of Major Suleimana, Rawlings now heard the Public Prosecutor doing the job for him by publicly quoting him word for word.

As Mr Aikins explained it to the court, Rawlings' principal motivation had been a desire to restore the image of the Armed Forces by getting them to use their final weeks in power to clear up the 'widespread corruption in high places' and to investigate the 'nefarious activities' of those Syrian and Lebanese businessmen who controlled most of the country's wholesale and import trade and who had been 'growing fat' at the expense of the starving masses. The rank and file within the court began to warm to Rawlings' theme.

The Public Prosecutor then went on to explain that in the course of some passionate argument with the hostage officers in the early hours of 15 May, Rawlings had said that if the military did not act immediately to 'cleanse the system' then the only solution that remained would be to 'go the Ethiopian way'. At this, the court erupted into wild cheering. The Ethiopian Head of State, Mengistu Haile Mariam, was a popular figure in African radical circles in those days and the cheering soldiers saw 'the Ethiopian way' as a clear reference to Mengistu's summary execution of hundreds of perceived opponents of the Ethiopian 'revolution' in 1977.

The court was adjourned for two days, but the die had been cast. By the time the court reopened on Wednesday 30 May, posters had begun appearing all over Burma Camp calling for the halting of the trial and the immediate release of Rawlings and his men. Some threatened death for the officers of the court while others openly called for nothing less than outright revolution.

During the course of evidence that day it was revealed that, at the time of his surrender, Rawlings had called for the release of the men under his command on the grounds that they were only acting on his express orders. He accepted full responsibility for the events of 15 May. The court was once more disrupted by wild cheering from the ranks. Rawlings had struck a popular chord in the imagination of the long-oppressed rank and file for this was the first time that an officer leading a failed coup had actually accepted responsibility for his actions and, in so doing, had sought to exonerate his men. Here was a real leader, a hero, an officer of integrity who could offer them inspiration. The next morning the *Daily Graphic* splashed across its front page the banner headline, 'Leave my men alone!' and from then on it was only a matter of time before Rawlings was forcibly released from gaol.

The move came in the early hours of Monday 4 June. The tension was so great that someone in Burma Camp performed the ritualist act of shooting himself. The next moment the whole place erupted. The first Rawlings knew of it was at 5.30 a.m. when a handful of men smashed the lock on his cell door in Special Branch headquarters. His rescuers proposed shooting the guards who had been holding him, but Rawlings, in an action that was to typify his attitude in the months ahead, said no, leave them alone, they were only doing their job. The soldiers then ran with him to nearby Broadcasting House which had already been seized by men of Fifth Battalion and Rawlings made that famous first public broadcast to the nation. It was an impassioned plea for calm in the midst of a highly-charged and explosive situation. In a state of breathless excitement, he shouted into the microphone:

> This is Flight Lieutenant Rawlings. The ranks have just got me out of my prison cell. In other words, the ranks have just taken over the destiny of this country. Fellow officers, if we are to avoid any bloodshed, I plead with you not to attempt to stand in their way because they are full of malice, hatred – hatred we have forced into them through all these years of suppression. They are ready to get it out – the venom we have created. So, for heaven's sake do not stand in their way. They are not fools. If you have any reason to fear them, you may run. If you have no reason to feel guilt, do not move . . . We can't restrain them.

Rawlings requested all units to send representatives to the new Revolutionary Council that would replace the SMC and he then gave crucial reassurance to the civilian population: 'The Ghana Armed forces will be handing over to the civilians in due time. Elections will take place.' How that was to be guaranteed was far from certain at the time. It simply reflected Rawlings' own feelings about what was fair and just. For the moment he recognised that the initiative lay with the military rank and file and, reflecting their feelings, he ominously warned: 'But before the elections go on, justice which has been denied to the Ghanaian worker will have to take place . . . Some of us have suffered for far too long.'

Then he uttered the famous phrase that was to become one of the key slogans of the revolution: 'You are either a part of the problem or part of the solution. There is no middle way.'

He went on to appeal to the officers that he knew would be needed if any control was to be established over the forces that were now unleashed:

> If you think you have worked for the welfare of your subordinates, you have nothing to fear . . . We know those among us who are honest, some even within the SMC . . . So for heaven's sake, do not run away. Be the men that you are and come to work. Come to Burma Camp. Nicholson Stadium will be our meeting ground where our elections will take place. Those who are looking out for our welfare will be elected . . . Elected leaders will now emerge, not those imposed on us.

Rawlings read out a list of specific junior officers and ranks who were to report to Burma Camp immediately. These were people whom he knew and trusted for, if he was to play anything like a leading part in the subsequent events, he would need all the help that he could get. He also called to Burma Camp a number of prominent civilians and Church leaders from whom he hoped to get advice.

It should be noted that Rawlings at this stage was uncertain about his own position in this emerging revolution. He was certainly not 'the leader of the coup'. His rescue had been the focal point that prompted the initial uprising. But what had now developed was a spontaneous revolution of the lower ranks against established authority. To some extent Rawlings himself was part of that authority structure. What would happen next was anybody's guess. It says much for Rawlings' strength of personality and his depth of understanding of the aspirations of the rank and file, that he was eventually able to establish some sort of order out of the initial chaos that struck the country on that fateful 4 June.

As Rawlings was escorted back to Burma Camp by members of the Fifth Battalion, they came under fire from the men of Recce Regiment. It was clear that the Recce 'boys' were still responding to the orders of their commanding officer and as a result desultory fighting continued throughout the morning between elements of the Recce Regiment on the one hand and the Fifth Battalion and Air Force on the other. At one stage the Army Commander, Major-General Odartey Wellington, regained control of Broadcasting House and called on all ranks to return to their barracks. Soon after leaving Broadcasting House, however, Odartey Wellington was killed in action and resistance to the revolution began to fall apart.

Some time after 3.00 p.m. the Chief of the Defence Staff, Major-General Joshua Hamidu, identifying himself firmly with the uprising, announced on the radio that the forces of the revolution had prevailed and 'the hypocrisy of the Acheampong and Akuffo regimes' was at an end. Repeating Rawlings' initial assurance that elections would go ahead as planned, he explained that the current revolution was 'in the national interest', adding, 'we have suffered for far too long.'

Rawlings, meanwhile, after some initial direct involvement in the fighting on the ground, had taken up an armed aircraft with the intention of blowing up Police Headquarters which was being used as a centre of resistance. Before he could reach his objective, however, his plane came under intense fire and was badly damaged. It was only his skill as a pilot combined with some luck that enabled him to land the plane and step out of it safely.

He took to the air again in a helicopter in order to keep track of what was happening on the ground. At one point he asked to be put down near Legon where he heard of Odartey Wellington's offer of peace talks. He sent the helicopter back to find out what was going on. For some reason the helicopter failed to return to the pre-arranged spot and for a few hours Rawlings was separated from the fighting. He remembers that during the afternoon the heavens opened with a welcome shower of rain. It seemed symbolic of a new awakening. Later he met someone who told him of Hamidu's broadcast. The day had been won.

Deciding it was too dangerous to move through the curfewed city during the hours of dusk and darkness, Rawlings stayed out in the bush and spent the night in the servant's quarters of a nearby house. He made his way to Air Force Station the following morning where he found Captain Boakye Djan drawing up on a blackboard a list of names for the new Revolutionary Council that was being formed. In the room were most of the junior officers and ranks whom Rawlings had named the day before and although he sensed a certain hostility from Boakye Djan, Rawlings was elected Chairman of the Council by general acclamation. The rest of the fifteen-man 'Armed Forces Revolutionary Council' (AFRC) was made up of a careful balance of junior and middle-ranking officers and representatives of the lower ranks.

While Rawlings and his companions were sorting out the details of the new governing body, outside on the streets of Accra groups of armed soldiers were ransacking shops and selected business premises. Any looting that went on was regarded by the soldiers involved as a justifiable 'redistribution of wealth'. Shops containing expensive imported luxuries had their goods methodically smashed to pieces while Lebanese businessmen were particularly singled out for individual assault and harassment. Impromptu roadblocks were set up throughout Accra and some civilians who were stopped, had a rifle pushed in their window and were faced with the demand: 'Are you part of the problem or part of the solution?' It was the sort of question to which there was only one possible answer!

Meanwhile, other soldiers were busy arresting all the senior officers they could lay their hands on and subjecting them to systematic humiliation, starting with the shaving of their heads.

Rawlings recognised the explosive situation for what it was. The men, he knew, wanted nothing more for the moment than to go on a vengeful levelling campaign – slaughtering all those officers and Military Intelligence men who had been humiliating them for years. Thus a major preoccupation for Rawlings in the weeks to come was how to harness the intense passions that had been unleashed by 4 June and direct it for doing good, rather than letting it waste itself in random and destructive acts of vengeance. It is noteworthy that in Rawlings' first official broadcast to the nation as Chairman of the AFRC, on the evening of Tuesday 5 June, the main focus of his short address was a direct appeal to the military rank and file to stop the indiscriminate molestation of their officers. There were, he assured them, many 'clean, disciplined, dedicated, radical, action-orientated' officers in the armed forces and all of them would be needed in the weeks ahead 'to assist us save and restore the integrity of this country'.

Rawlings recognised that he had no experience in the day-to-day affairs of government, so that night he sought the advice of a handful of those clean and trusted senior officers he had referred to in his broadcast: Lieutenant-General Joshua Hamidu, Brigadier Joseph Nunoo-Mensah and Group Captain Frank Okyne. These three, at least, were thus saved the ignominy of having their heads shaved.

'That young man has asked us to form a government,' General Hamidu remarked to his two colleagues with an air of patronising contentment. Hamidu was anxious to salvage some kind of role for the senior officer corps and from his point of view, it was their duty to relieve Flight Lieutenant Rawlings of as much responsibility as possible. At the same time Hamidu felt that in the long-term interests of the military hierarchy, the senior officer corps should divest itself of the sort of total control of government which it had exercised in Acheampong's time. Civilians should be more fully involved in the top levels of government. The economist Dr J. L. S. Abbey, Commissioner for Finance in the Akuffo government, was brought in on these discussions and he recommended that, for the sake of administrative stability, the civilians of the previous government should be left in place at the head of the various ministries. This, he argued, would leave Rawlings and the AFRC free to decide on policy directives and to control the precarious military situation. Rawlings acted on this advice and appointed General Hamidu as Liaison Officer between the ministries and the AFRC – in effect a sort of 'Prime Minister' – a position which Hamidu exploited to the full. Seeing himself as an important balancing factor in the uncertain times ahead, Hamidu moved into the Castle, the official seat of government, while Rawlings was based in Burma Camp throughout the period of AFRC rule.

The soldiers responded to Rawlings' second broadcast and over the next couple of days their activities on the streets quietened down considerably. The AFRC called the presidential candidates from the various political parties to a meeting on 7 June to reassure them that they had nothing to fear from the military's 'house cleaning' exercise. After some discussion it was agreed that the parliamentary and presidential elections would proceed as arranged on 18 June, but that the handover of power would be postponed for three months to 1 October to allow the AFRC to complete its task. This left Rawlings free to concentrate his energy on what he saw as the main focus of the June 4th Revolution: the clearing up of corruption in all walks of life and in particular the *kalabule* system which had for so many years directly affected the cost of living in the market-place.

An immediate attack was made upon the *kalabule* traders when it was announced that henceforth all goods were to be sold at their official controlled prices. In many cases this was a fraction of the prices actually being charged in the market. Concentrating on this end of the *kalabule* chain was dealing with the symptoms rather than the cause of the disease, but it was believed that if retailers were forced to sell at low, controlled prices, then they would refuse to pay *kalabule* prices to the middle-men who, in turn, would pass the new 'realism' up the line to the producer. With any luck many middle-men would be cut out altogether as retailers would be forced to go straight to the producer. This was the theory. The immediate practice was that many goods were withdrawn from the market. Soldiers reacted to this by going on a campaign against those whom they accused of hoarding. Throughout Accra and other major cities, hoarded goods were confiscated and sold to the public at controlled prices, store-houses were destroyed and several market women were flogged in public.

The revolution's prices and anti-hoarding policy and its crude attempts to bring law and order to the market-place culminated on 18 August in the clearing of Makola No 1 Market in the centre of Accra before its symbolic destruction with high explosives. This event, however, was more like a final act in the anti-*kalabule* drama. Long before then, in the first few weeks of the revolution, a new realism had entered the public consciousness, a new popular willingness to embrace wholeheartedly the moral aspirations of the revolution. For those not already jubilant supporters from the beginning, the public executions of 16 June evoked a general awareness that this regime was not like any other: it meant business.

From the civilian point of view, the early weeks of the revolution consisted of soldiers enforcing price controls – a policy which the poorer mass of the population welcomed with enthusiasm, even if they had some reservations about the arbitrary and often violent nature of the soldiers' methods. What most did not appreciate was the struggle going on behind the scenes.

The most urgent practical crisis facing Rawlings and the officers of the AFRC throughout the month of June was controlling the vengeful anarchy of the general soldiery. It was very much *their* revolution and initially the rank and file expected to be able to shoot all officers over the rank of captain. It was known that there was in circulation a list of 207 senior officers who were to be executed immediately. Those like Rawlings, who appreciated the anger and frustration of the men, feared that once the killing started it would be almost impossible to stop. On several occasions during that first ten days Rawlings virtually lost control of the situation. While Boakye Djan devised delaying tactics, Rawlings tried suggesting that those found guilty of corruption or abuse of power should be sentenced to lengthy terms of imprisonment with hard labour. They could perform the useful tasks of weeding, clearing up and generally rejuvenating the many long-neglected state farms in the country. But the merest hint of such an alternative aroused suspicions among some that Rawlings himself was losing his revolutionary ardour.

On Monday 11 June six execution stakes were mounted at Teshie firing range, opposite the Military Academy near the Tema road. This was before any formal military court had even been assembled. The principal officers of the previous regime were clearly already condemned in the eyes of the ranks and in this they had the full support of the country's university students. The following day a large body of students from the University of Ghana marched from Legon to Burma Camp waving posters which demanded: 'Firing squad for nation wreckers' and 'Let the blood flow!'

The primary target was Acheampong. He was brought to Accra and confronted with the allegations levelled against him since July 1978, namely that he had abused power for his own selfish ends and ruined the country generally. Acheampong was given a televised press conference in which to answer his accusers. It was subsequently claimed by some within the AFRC that the press conference was authorised to give Acheampong the opportunity to show repentance and remorse, and thus help defuse the vengeful mood within the ranks. If that was the intention, then he was not properly prepared for Acheampong was arrogant to the point of recklessness. He showed no remorse and strenuously denied allegations of secret bank accounts and large personal land-holdings. He argued instead that he had been too kind to people like Akuffo whom he then went on to implicate in numerous acts of bribery and corruption. He appeared not to realise that this was the nearest he was ever likely to get to a public trial. Some argue in retrospect that had Acheampong expressed some remorse, revealed his alleged Swiss bank account and undertaken to return all the money he had stolen, he may have saved his own life. This is unlikely. A sacrifice in blood was demanded and if the vengeful soldiery were to be controlled at all, somebody had to symbolically pay the ultimate penalty for all that had gone before.

On Saturday 16 June it was announced that Acheampong and General Utuka, the former Commander of the Border

Guard, had been executed by firing squad at Teshie firing range. The execution had taken place soon after 6.00 a.m., in full view of the public road between Tema and Accra and watched by a few curious passers-by. There was a precedent for public execution at Teshie firing range. In 1967 two junior officers had suffered a similar fate for leading an abortive coup in which General E. K. Kotoka had been killed. But the execution of a former Head of State was unprecedented in Ghana and it caused quite a stir in the country and abroad. Significantly, there was no outright condemnation of the executions by Church, media, lawyers or other professional bodies. Most Ghanaians seem to have accepted that some blood letting was inevitable in the circumstances. For the moment the attention of many was turned to the general election on the Monday.

To the admitted surprise of most foreign observers, the parliamentary and presidential elections took place on schedule in conditions of amazing calm and fairness. For the rest of that week people were absorbed in the outcome of the election as more results were published every day. By Friday 22 June it was clear that the PNP had won a narrow overall majority. There was no clear winner in the presidential election and a second round run-off between the PNP's Dr Hilla Limann and the PFP's Victor Owusu was scheduled for 9 July.

During election week the late Major-General Odartey Wellington was honoured with a formal state funeral because, in Rawlings' view, even though the former Army Commander had died opposing the uprising of 4 June, he was an honourable man who had bravely given his life for the protection of the state. The funeral was a symbolic gesture which Rawlings hoped would quell the cries for further blood and restore some badly-needed respect for the senior officer corps.

With the elections successfully out of the way, however, the attention of the students and the ranks returned to the matter at hand – the next round of executions. Over the weekend students held noisy demonstrations demanding further executions. Rawlings was in a near impossible situation in that the salvation of the officer corps as a whole depended on the flow of more blood in order to appease the anger. By the Sunday there were rumours in Accra that Rawlings would be removed if he tried to stem the flow of 'people's justice'. On Monday 25 June a lone voice spoke out against the trend. Elizabeth Ohene, Literary Editor of the *Graphic*, published an article in which she argued that 'Death [was]not the answer'. She condemned the macabre slogan of the times, 'Let the blood flow!', and argued that any further executions would merely serve to brutalize the general citizenry. The students responded by invading the *Graphic* offices in Accra and daubing the walls with slogans such as 'Death to Ohene!' Fortunately Ohene was not in the building. Rawlings, by contrast, appreciated her brave stand and recommended her promotion to the editorship of the *Graphic*. Ohene, however, asserted the independence of the press under the new constitution by declining to accept the position from the Head of State. She agreed instead to become Acting Editor on a temporary basis until the new Press Commission was promulgated and functioning.

Behind the scenes Rawlings and the other officers of the AFRC were struggling to control the situation. But it was clear that another round of executions was on the way. The next six victims were assembled and, with no legal representation for their defence, they were briefly tried before the special secret courts which had been hastily set up over the weekend. Rawlings signed the death warrants, knowing that if he failed to do so he would lose control of the situation and then things would really fall apart. Subsequent attempts by Rawlings and other middle-ranking officers to postpone the executions were of no avail. There was a three-hour delay at the firing range on the morning of Tuesday 26 June as the officers present argued over procedure. With no officer willing to give the final order, they employed delaying tactics hoping to postpone the execution altogether. At one point Lieutenant Smith appeared and the execution squad observed with apprehension the heated discussions taking place between Smith and the other officers. The men must have sensed it was an attempt to stop 'the action' and they would not be held back. At 9.00 a.m., with tension mounting, someone from the ranks shouted 'Fire!' and the deed was done. A volley of shots rang out to enthusiastic cheers from the large crowd that had gathered by the roadside.

Among those executed that day were two more former Heads of State, General A.A. Afrifa (1969) and General Fred Akuffo (1978-9). With them were Air Vice-Marshal G.Y. Boakye, Rear-Admiral Joy Amedume, former Chief of Defence Staff, General R.E.A. Kotei, and former Commissioner for Foreign Affairs, Colonel Roger Felli.

Those not carried away by vengeful instincts were visibly shocked by this second round of executions. The following morning Ohene returned to the fray, calling upon the Churches and professional bodies to 'Stand up and be counted' by stating their positions on the executions and the arbitrary floggings in the market-place. The Churches finally responded with a cautiously-worded statement which expressed concern about the secrecy of the trials. The Ghana Bar Association followed suit with a condemnation of the secret trials, the 'summary executions' and the indiscriminate floggings.

The most turbulent month in Ghana's history ended with a dawn broadcast in which Rawlings announced that there would be no more executions. Further people found guilty of corruption would face long prison sentences. By the time of this broadcast Rawlings appears to have regained the initiative and secured some kind of control of the situation. The students were not satisfied, but they now had a new focus for their anger: Nigeria.

Foreign governments had been quick to condemn the second spate of executions, especially neighbouring African states, many of whose military dictators had reason to fear a similar eruption of the lower ranks in their own country. Nigeria's General Obasanjo was particularly concerned as he was going through just the sort of precarious transition to civilian rule that his 'brother Akuffo' had been engaged in. In addition, as the 'super power' of the region, Nigerians generally considered themselves responsible for directing the destiny of their neighbours. Thus Nigeria reacted to Ghana's second round of executions by immediately cutting off the country's oil supplies. Since Ghana received 80 per cent of her crude oil from Nigeria, this was a hard blow indeed. But Ghanaians reacted with superb defiance.

If there had been any doubts about wholehearted support for the revolution, these were now banished by the sense of national solidarity which was aroused by Nigeria's oil embargo. Strict petrol and diesel rationing was introduced and public transport disappeared from the roads; yet people willingly walked miles to their place of work. As food stocks began to run low in the cities through lack of transport from the rural areas, the people's spirit was still not dampened and they did not blame the revolution for their hardship. The students of the University of Ghana marched through Accra on a seven-hour demonstration during which they pledged support for the secret trials and condemned all foreign pressure, proclaiming on their placards, 'Nigeria hoard your oil – we shall clean our house!' and 'A half revolution is no revolution!' Hardship seemed to strengthen the Ghanaian resolve and demonstrations expressing similar support for the revolution were held in other cities.

Further secret trials began on 11 July and over the next two months a wide range of military personnel and some civilians were handed down long prison sentences for the corrupt amassing of wealth during the SMC regimes. The trial of the first three accused lasted barely one day, after which they were sentenced to 50 years, 80 years and 95 years respectively! The extraordinary length of prison sentences was no doubt partly symbolic, to reassure those still demanding blood that prison was not a soft option and at the same time to serve as a warning to future rulers of the country. A corrupt Commissioner for Foreign Affairs was sentenced to 150 years, but, more typically, sentences from the Special Courts were for 5, 10, 15 years or 'life'.

The AFRC was determined that the government of the Third Republic should not undo or undermine the actions and achievements of the revolution. With this in mind they had already added a set of special clauses to the new constitution before its official promulgation on 14 June. In the first place these 'Transitional Provisions' indemnified all those involved in staging the coup of 4 June. In the second place they ruled that it would be unconstitutional for any subsequent government to alter or retract any official action taken in the name of the AFRC, including in particular, the judgements of the Special Courts.

On 9 July, Dr Hilla Limann won the second round of presidential elections by a large majority over his opponent Victor Owusu. There then began a curious relationship between Limann and the AFRC as both prepared for the forthcoming transfer of power. Limann was briefed by Hamidu on the state of the country and a Joint Planning Commission was set up to liaise on policy matters. Limann accepted the Transitional Provisions which the AFRC had added to the constitution. In fact he went out of his way to state publicly that he would not revoke any action taken by the AFRC, adding, 'I am not a man of half measures'.

At the end of August Rawlings announced in a nationwide broadcast that since he was so confident that the 'house cleaning' operation would be continued by Limann and the incoming PNP government, the AFRC would be handing over power a week early, on Monday 24 September. In the meantime Rawlings went to Cuba to represent Ghana at the Non-Aligned Movement (NAM) summit conference. He felt it was important that he should explain to the other non-aligned countries the aims and aspirations of the Ghanaian revolution. The Cubans expressed surprise that the Ghanaian leader had agreed to hand power back to a crowd of bourgeois civilian politicians, and when Rawlings was departing from Havana military headquarters, Fidel Castro's brother offered him a small hand machine-gun, remarking that if he handed over power, he would be needing it. At the time Rawlings felt that the Cubans were over-reacting and that they did not understand the Ghanaian situation. Years later he was to reflect that perhaps they understood only too well.

On the eve of handover Rawlings had reason to be proud of the achievements of the June 4th Revolution. In purely economic terms the achievement of the AFRC's brief term in office was impressive. Their methods may have been crude, and Rawlings constantly had to rein in and apologise for the excesses of the soldiery, but there is no doubt that the AFRC slashed inflation almost instantly, bringing prices down to 'more tolerable levels'. At the same time they raised the official prices paid to farmers, to encourage agricultural production. The cocoa price in particular went up by 50 per cent and the entire upper hierarchy of the Cocoa Marketing Board (CMB) was replaced. Several companies had their assets seized by the state on account of trade malpractices and numerous foreign businessmen, mainly Lebanese, were deported for being involved in illegal deals. A special commission was set up to investigate unpaid taxes and huge amounts of money were recovered for the government. Similarly, strenuous efforts were made to collect unpaid debts owed to state corporations. In monetary terms, an initial estimate of twenty-three million cedis was brought into government coffers during this short three-month period; but more significant in the long term was the awakening of a new tax consciousness among the Ghanaian people. In effect, the AFRC's energetic exposure and prosecution of tax evasion and financial fraud was a precursor for the work of the Citizens' Vetting Committee of 1982.

For Rawlings, the greatest achievement of the June 4th Revolution was the awakening of the spirit of the people. Rawlings himself was wildly popular. Wherever he went people flocked to see and to cheer this hero who had burst so suddenly into their lives. 'JJ! JJ!' they shouted as they clamoured around him. Here was a leader who had defied established authority and set himself so firmly on the side of the suffering masses. From Rawlings' own point of view, and that of anyone who understood the times, however, it was anything but a one-man show. Rawlings flavoured the character of the revolution. His personality and style were a dominant characteristic of the period, but they were symbolic of a much deeper awakening.

Although Rawlings had appointed Boakye Djan as spokesman for the Council on the grounds that he himself was not used to public speaking, in fact when it came to it, Rawlings himself did most of the speaking. Much of his energy and activity in those frenetic months was bound up with talking to the people: in quiet rooms, in formal interviews, in market places, on roadsides and from the roof of a Landrover or armoured vehicle. Over and over again in his speeches throughout the country, Rawlings constantly urged the people to be aware that this was *their* revolution. It was *they* who were calling their past rulers to account. The future of Ghana was in *their* hands.

Looking back on the three-and-a-half months of AFRC rule, Rawlings summed up his interpretation of the revolution in an emotional broadcast to the nation on his last evening in office:

> We have all been witnesses to the decay in our sick society; for too long our dear country has known

> nothing better than the greedy lust for power and the wicked use of power to entrench privilege among a few in our society. Social conscience had fled our rulers; ... Ghana had achieved independent status only to be held to ransom by a succession of selfish individuals ... Mother Ghana was groaning in agony.
>
> ... On 4th June 1979, we, the young officers of the armed forces and the other ranks, rose up in spontaneous mutiny to remove the causes of so much national pollution. Our immediate task was to cleanse the armed forces, which had lost its bearings in the wilderness of indiscipline and unprofessional behaviour. But our fundamental and long-term aim was to launch a revolution which would cleanse the whole nation, turn the hearts and minds of our people against social injustices and ultimately redirect the pattern of our national life ...
>
> We have done our best in this short space of time to throw a searching light into the dark recesses of corruption and malpractices in our country ...
>
> ...no one should mistake the sweeping force and dynamic energy of our revolution of social conscience ...

Rawlings admitted that the AFRC's revolution in public consciousness had only scratched the surface of the nation's problems, but it was a beginning: the seeds had been sown. Meanwhile, he and his colleagues in the AFRC would 'go back to our vocation in the armed forces, ready to work to assist the incoming government with our modest efforts.'

As a result of the June 4th interregnum Ghanaians faced the new era of the Third Republic with a far greater sense of hope and expectation for the future than they had felt for many years.

Chapter 3

The Civilian Interregnum

On 24 September 1979 the Third Republic of Ghana was formally inaugurated in Parliament House, Accra. Rawlings made a short speech before handing over to his successor, Dr Limann. It was by far the most memorable speech of the day. He reminded the assembled members of parliament and dignitaries of the appalling state the country had been in before 4 June, emphasising that while the people of Ghana were suffering from lack of food, poor health services, exorbitant rents and the effects of rampant inflation, 'there were others in society who were dipping their hands freely into the nation's coffers so that they and their families could live in the opulence of conspicuous consumption.' He spoke of the achievements of the AFRC in clearing up this corrupt state of affairs and replenishing the government's coffers, but most of all he emphasised the 'new consciousness of the people' which had been awakened by the June 4th Revolution and which would hold any future government to account.

'Never lose sight of this new consciousness of the Ghanaian people,' Rawlings warned Limann:

> Never before have the eyes of so many been focused on so few, Mr President. The few are you, the illustrious members of our new civilian administration. The many are those in the factories and on the farms, in the dormitories and junior quarters

> who will be watching you, with eagles' eyes to see whether the change they are hoping for will actually materialise in their lifetime.

He concluded in the words which Limann was to take as nothing short of a veiled threat:

> We know you will deliver the goods. That is why we have turned a deaf ear to those who have entreated us to stay on a little longer, because our job is not complete. We have every confidence that we shall never regret our decision to go back to barracks.

Limann's reply was bland by comparison. He spoke in eloquent terms of the founding fathers of the nation, with whom he wished to associate his administration, emphasising in particular his party's inheritance from the Osagyefo, Dr Kwame Nkrumah. Limann was noncommittal on the specific plans of his government, promising merely to be 'open and honest, modest yet vigorous'. He pointedly avoided reference to his predecessor's government, mentioning the AFRC just once, to thank them for holding the elections that had enabled this handover to take place. It appeared that in his mind Ghanaians that day had drawn a line under the previous years of military rule and were returning once more to the familiar safety and security of the civilian fold. It was an optimistic assumption,

Following the inauguration ceremony, the new president, in his capacity as Commander-in-Chief of the Armed Forces, addressed a formal military parade in Independence Square. Rawlings by this time had already symbolically returned to take his place among the ranks on the parade ground. At the end of the march past, taking up the rear, came Flight Lieutenant Rawlings and Captain Boakye Djan, saluting all the way around the arena, to wildly enthusiastic cries of 'J.J.! J.J.!' from the public as they spotted him. The day had clearly belonged to Rawlings.

Dr Hilla Limann was a new and hitherto unknown figure in the national politics of Ghana. He had in fact been a compromise figure in the PNP's choice of candidate for presidential office. Their first choice had been the party's founder, Imoru Egala, but he had been excluded by a twelve-year bar from public office dating back to 1969. His appeal against the ban was still pending when the time came for nomination papers to be filed in April 1979.

Hilla Limann seemed an ideal alternative choice of candidate for the presidency. He was a northerner, from the Upper Region, a distinct advantage for the PNP in that it gave an otherwise southern oriented party greater national credibility. He was modest and unassuming and could be portrayed as a people's man for he came from humble origins and was known to have paid for his higher education abroad through his own hard work and savings. If academic qualifications were needed for the job, then Hilla Limann had them all. He had a BSc from the London School of Economics, a Master's in Constitutional Law and a Doctorate in Political Science from the University of Paris. As a civil servant he had been Ghana's representative at the International Labour Organisation and the World Health Organisation in Geneva. He had served on the constitutional committee which drafted proposals for the 1969 constitution and in the early months of 1979 he had acted as personal adviser and assistant to Imoru Egala in his work on the Constituent Assembly which drew up the constitution for the Third Republic. Limann's credentials were impeccable, and even the fact that he was unknown on the national political scene could be seen as an advantage for it meant that he was untainted by the sorry reputations of previous civilian governments.

Once Limann had been approved as presidential candidate by the party congress, the PNP's electoral machinery moved into top gear, well-oiled by the money of such wealthy patrons as Nana Okutwer Bekoe III, party chairman, Kojo Botsio, Dr Ayeh-Kumi, Kofi Batsa and others. The thoroughness of the PNP machine was all the more remarkable in that there had been no official party activity for more than seven years. But the CPP foundations had been well laid in the 1950s and early 60s and former 'Young Pioneers' from the Nkrumah era proved willing volunteers in getting people out to vote in the 1979 election. There were rumours at the time that PNP members were going round marginal constituencies spreading wild allegations and misleading illiterate villagers about their opponents. One story which circulated in 1979, and was revived in 1982 after the fall of the PNP, was that in at least one rural constituency the PNP had told voters that 18 June was the day for casting votes for the PNP only; supporters of other parties would vote the following day! The story has been vehemently denied by Dr Limann and others, but the power of rumour is such in Ghana that it is still widely believed more than a decade later. The international observers did not find anything untoward on voting day and many of the rumours of PNP malpractice may have arisen principally from a sense of despair among political opponents who had no answer to the widespread efficiency of the PNP (old CPP) electoral machine.

The very strength of the PNP machine, however, was in the long run to prove a liability for Limann once he had assumed office. Having no personal power-base of his own within the party, Limann became captive to those powerful party interests which had engineered his election and they expected some return on their investment. This limited Limann's ability to act with the full freedom of an effective executive president and his government quickly became bogged down with the strict adherence to the letter of the constitution which a constitutionalist like Limann insisted upon, combined with the behind-the-scenes machinations and personal rivalries of the unelected party bosses. Any fair assessment of Limann's administration must bear in mind these two crucial limitations.

The in-coming President and his administration had been put on notice by Rawlings' barely concealed threat in his handing-over speech. The civilian politicians who now took office had the immensely difficult task of not only governing the country through particularly difficult economic times, but also of proving the worthiness of civilian government *per se*. Rather than seek to prove their worth with dynamic and selfless government, however, the politicians of the Third Republic and their unelected party backers chose to safeguard their own futures by removing what they saw as the one major threat to their security: Rawlings and anyone associated with the AFRC. In doing so, they addressed themselves to the symptoms, not the cause of the disease of political instability. In turning a blind eye to the one factor which always ensured ready civilian acceptance of military intervention in African politics – poverty and despair combined with visible corruption in government – the civilian politicians of 1979 revealed that they had failed to learn the most rudimentary lessons of the June 4th Revolution.

Limann himself, however, recognised the importance of some aspects of the June 4th Revolution better than most of his colleagues. In his first few weeks in office he called for the setting up of non-partisan vigilante committees to safeguard against a revival of the *kalabule* abuses of hoarding, smuggling and selling above controlled prices. The vigilante groups, he hoped, would become a peaceful and controlled civilian alternative to the arbitrary acts of the military in the market places during the AFRC period. Ironically, the vigilante concept bore striking resemblance in principle to the People's Defence Committees (PDCs) set up in the wake of the 31 December revolution which overthrew Limann in 1981. But in October 1979 the idea received outright condemnation from Limann's fellow politicians, especially the lawyers among them, who saw it as a dangerous abrogation of power to the people, and the idea was quickly dropped.

In tackling the perceived problem of the 'threat' from the military, Limann was at the mercy of Military Intelligence who formed his only source of information about what was going on within the armed forces. It was on their advice that he acted to remove the AFRC personnel from direct contact with the armed forces. The officers were offered courses abroad, followed by gratuity and resettlement allowances. Those that chose not to accept these were encouraged to retire on substantial benefits. Rawlings refused both alternatives, rightly viewing any offer of a course or work abroad as a deliberate attempt to remove him from his self-appointed role as watchdog for the people. He even refused the profferred position of a seat on the Council of State.

Meanwhile people within the PNP began circulating rumours designed to discredit the achievements of the AFRC. Early in November 1979 Limann announced that the estimated ₵23 million, which the AFRC claimed to have collected, had never been handed over and the PNP had been left with nothing but debts. This provoked a sharp riposte from the AFRC's Special Tribunal which was still sitting under Justice I.K.Abban. He confirmed that ₵23 million was lodged in a special account in the Ghana Commercial Bank and that not a pesewa of it had been withdrawn by the AFRC. As soon as discussions with the Ministry of Finance and the Accountant General were complete, the whole amount would be transferred to the government's Consolidated Fund. Eventually Dr John Nabila, the Minister for Presidential Affairs, was to confirm in Parliament in January 1981 that a total of C36 million had been collected directly by the AFRC and handed over to the in-coming administration and that this was in addition to a further

₵168 million of taxes collected by the Central Revenue Department in the period July to August 1979.

Forces within the new administration, however, were determined to blacken the reputation of the AFRC. On 12 November 1979 five AFRC convicts escaped from Ussher Fort Prison. The escapees were officers of whom Rawlings was reputed to have said that they did not really deserve a gaol sentence and their imprisonment had been but a temporary expedient to lower the temper of 'the boys' in the heat of the revolution. Almost immediately, rumours began to circulate to the effect that Rawlings was in some way implicated in their escape from gaol. Rawlings responded with a press conference in which he vigorously denied the rumours: '... this is part of a campaign to discredit the government of the Armed Forces Revolutionary Council of which I was Chairman.'

Referring with contempt to the 'enemies of the June 4th Revolution' as 'the fat exploiters who resented everything the AFRC stood for', Rawlings claimed that since 24 September: '[they] have been leaving no stone unturned in their effort to reverse the gains that were made by the people of this country during our short period in office.'

Undaunted, Military Intelligence submitted a report to the President in which they claimed that the gaol-break had indeed been masterminded by Rawlings, as a diversion for a coup that was to have been led by Brigadier Quainoo the following morning. They never produced any evidence to substantiate their claim, nor did they account for why the alleged coup attempt did not take place.

For some weeks Limann had been bombarded with reports and rumours of coups and plots, and now this final one, combined with the actual escape from Ussher Prison, was enough to prompt him to action. He invited Rawlings to the Castle on the occasion of the swearing in of the Council of State on Tuesday 27 November. While Rawlings was in the Castle, it was announced on the radio that he had been retired from the Air Force with immediate effect on the grounds that his 'continued presence in the Armed Forces as a serving officer is incompatible with his former status'. Rawlings did not learn about it himself until he got home that night to be told by his wife who had heard it on the radio. He was flabbergasted and very bitter about the way it had been done behind his back, but in a spirit of determination to prove the worth of respect for authority, he accepted the retirement, without an official complaint.

The following morning the newspapers carried the news under banner headlines, together with the announcement that the key AFRC appointees, Brigadier Joseph Nunoo-Mensah, Chief of Defence Staff, Brigadier Arnold Quainoo, Army Commander, and Mr C.O.Lamptey, Inspector General of Police, had all been similarly retired. On its inside page the *Daily Graphic* headed the story with a photograph of Rawlings in the Castle the previous evening, smiling and talking with Limann, with the caption: 'Prominent among those who were present at the ceremony was Flight Lieutenant Jerry Rawlings who was yesterday retired from the Armed Forces.' The clear implication was that Rawlings happily accepted a retirement of which, at that stage, he had not even been informed. It certainly had all the hallmarks of a clever and carefully staged piece of government propaganda.

Not content with engineering the sacking of the principal officers of the AFRC, the security services proceeded to harass them and anyone connected with them during their time in office. Over the next two years Rawlings was perpetually watched and followed and those of his friends within the ranks who visited him at his flat were warned off by Military Intelligence. Numerous privates and NCOs who had been active with the AFRC were dismissed from the forces. Captain Kojo Tsikata (rtd.), a known left-wing sympathiser who had offered informal advice to the AFRC, was openly followed by men from Military Intelligence and

Special Branch who, on one occasion, went so far as to force his car off the road in what can only be described as an attempt to kill or seriously injure him. At the same time Brigadier Quainoo was banned from entering Burma Camp or the Military Academy where he had been seen talking with soldiers who were even forbidden to accept lifts in the car of their former Army Commander. If the security services argued that Rawlings and the sympathisers of the AFRC were a danger to the state, they were certainly going the right way about ensuring that their prophecies would come true.

While all this was going on, strenuous efforts were being made by certain lawyers to reverse the decisions of the AFRC's Special Courts – those which were supposedly protected by the Transitional Provisions of the constitution. It began in mid-November 1979 when Justice K.E.Amua-Sekyi of the Accra High Court granted bail to three AFRC convicts pending their appeal against sentence. The three freed convicts promptly fled the country. To Limann's credit, the state appealed against this ruling on the grounds that it was contrary to the Transitional Provisions of the constitution which could only be interpreted by the Supreme Court. Limann knew his constitutional law. He also knew the mood within the country at the time that the AFRC's Special Courts had been sitting. He saw the whole issue as political dynamite and he begged his legal friends to let the matter rest, at least until the next election when the question of the repeal of the Transitional Provisions could be put to the electorate.

The three Justices of the Appeal Court, Annie Jiagge, E.N.P.Sowah and P.E.N.K.Archer, agreed with Limann's interpretation and referred the matter to the Supreme Court. But other judges would not let the matter lie. In July 1980 Mrs Justice Cecilia Koranteng Addow granted the Habeas Corpus application of AFRC convict Lloyd Shackleford. He was subsequently set free on the grounds that he was 'never tried'. Other attempts to overturn the sentences of the AFRC courts were made during 1980 and several more prisoners were set free.

In February 1981 a trial case was brought before the Supreme Court but after two days of hearings, the Court decided to reserve judgement. While the most senior judges in the land hesitated to make a ruling on the matter, Limann spoke out firmly against any attempt by members of parliament to tamper with the Transitional Provisions. The Supreme Court case was reopened in June 1981 and Rawlings was summoned as a witness. In the light of Rawlings' assurance that all the AFRC convicts had indeed been tried, according to the Special Courts, five Supreme Court judges, including Chief Justice Apaloo, concluded that even though the AFRC trials may have been 'a breach of natural justice', they could not intervene against them because of the Transitional Provisions. Nevertheless, in spite of this ruling, over the following months other High Court judges released most of the remaining AFRC convicts on various legal technicalities.

Although Limann was clearly unhappy with what was going on, he was powerless to intervene as the constitution was quite specific on the strict independence of the Judiciary. The state-owned *Daily Graphic* probably reflected the thinking of senior government ministers when it commented in an editorial: 'To the average person who stopped screaming for the flow of more blood on the understanding that AFRC decisions [would] not be touched by any Court, it all sounds very puzzling.' To the supporters of the principles of the AFRC, it all sounded very much like a deliberate undermining of the June 4th Revolution.

For all their provocative acts against the AFRC and its associates, the politicians of the Third Republic may yet have survived until the next election if they had achieved more in the way of sorting out the economy, had demonstrated more clearly that they cared for the plight of the ordinary Ghanaian and had set a better example as rulers of the country.

The economic situation that the Limann administration inherited in September 1979 was teetering on the brink of national crisis. The AFRC's hammering of consumer prices, following on from the currency exchange of the Akuffo government, had succeeded in reducing inflation quite dramatically. But once the hammer of the AFRC was lifted, there was little beyond wishful thinking to prevent inflation from soaring once again. The AFRC had been too briefly in office to develop any policy of tackling the fundamental problems of underproduction and unemployment. The economic advisers to the PNP seem to have relied upon the naïve belief that AFRC surplus funds would enable them to go on an importation binge in their first few months in office and so, by flooding the market with consumer goods, satisfy pre-election promises and somehow curb inflation. In practice, not only was the necessary foreign exchange not available, but flooding the market would only have created a temporary illusion of prosperity. In the long run it would have done little more than open up opportunities for a renewal of *kalabule* corruption.

As it was, the first one hundred days of the Limann administration was characterised by an air of inactivity. It took several months to assemble a team of ministers that would pass the approval of parliament. There was still one ministerial appointment outstanding by Christmas. The one sector of the economy that formed the basis for any long-term economic stability and growth was agriculture and yet it was six months before the government came up with any major agricultural programme. Even then, beyond bringing more land into state ownership, most of the plan seemed to consist of declarations of government intent to treat agriculture as a priority. It was not until the end of 1981 that any decisive action was taken to help the individual farmer with a serious increase in producer prices for export crops. In mid-1980 J.H.Mensah, former Minister of Finance in Busia's government and founding member of the PFP, warned that it was 'a dangerous piece of folly for the government to underestimate the seriousness of the present food situation in the country.'

Meanwhile, inflation was soaring, to 70 per cent in 1980 and 100 per cent in 1981. The minimum wage of four cedis a day was raised to ten cedis and finally to twelve cedis in November 1980, but then in July 1981, when presenting his budget to parliament, the Minister of Finance had the political insensitivity to blame the spiralling inflation on the rise in minimum wage levels, at a time when government ministers were earning ₵4300 a month, with huge expense allowances.

That particular budget was defeated – a unique event in the parliamentary history of independent Ghana. It was an indication of Parliament's lack of confidence in the government's record on the economy, which derived from a failure to balance government finances, falling agricultural production, loss of confidence in the cedi and unacceptably high inflation, all in the face of the intolerable hardships being faced by the vast majority of Ghanaians. A revised set of budget proposals was finally approved by Parliament in August 1981, but, significantly, these failed to include any symbolic cut in the high expense allowances awarded to ministers and members of Parliament.

In retrospect, ministers have spoken of the problems of working with a civil service not used to the confines of a strict constitution. One minister recalled having a copy of the constitution permanently on his desk for consultation every time he had to take a decision. There was no back-up from a civil service more attuned to the free-wheeling system of ministerial decree. Other members of the Limann administration have protested that military intervention on 31 December 1981 deprived them of the opportunity to prove the long-term worth of their evolving policies.

The public perception of those years, however, was

1 Independence Arch
Anna Tully/PANOS Pictures

2 Hands off Africa! Africa must be free! Nkrumah addressing the All African Peoples' Conference, December 1958
Ministry of Information

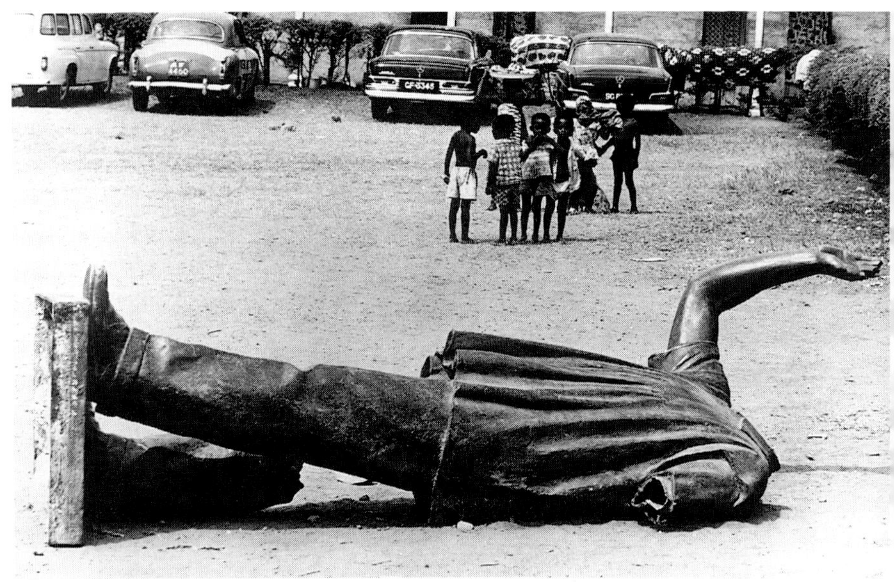

3 The Fall of Nkrumah, February 1966

Camera Press

4 Flight Lieutenant Rawlings and his co-conspirators face the Military Tribunal, Burma Camp, May 1979

People's Daily Graphic

5 Students demonstrating in support of the June 4th Revolution
People's Daily Graphic

6 Chairman of the AFRC, J.J. Rawlings, addressing the students
People's Daily Graphic

7 Flight Lieutenant Rawlings confers with Captain Boakye Djan at an AFRC press conference, June 1979

Teresa Coleman/Camera Press

8 The execution site, Teshie firing range, June 1979

People's Daily Graphic

9 Dr Hilla Limann, the PNP's presidential candidate, on the campaign trail, June 1979
Teresa Coleman/Camera Press

10 J.J. Rawlings queuing to cast his vote, 18 June 1979
People's Daily Graphic

11 Chairman of the AFRC in consultation with market women

Ministry of Information

12 The destruction of Makola Market, August 1979

People's Daily Graphic

13 The Chairman of the AFRC, J.J. Rawlings, hands over power to the President of the Third Republic, Dr Hilla Limann

People's Daily Graphic

14 'Holy War' declared, 31 December 1981

Popperfoto

15 Workers' demonstration in support of the 'Holy War'

People's Daily Graphic

16 Flight Lieutenant Jerry Rawlings explaining the aims of the 31 December revolution to a crowd at Nicholson Stadium, Burma Camp, 8 January 1982

Associated Press

primarily one of poverty and hardship for the majority, contrasted with the wealth and self-satisfaction of the élite. The disillusionment of the workers and the unemployed was reflected in the widespread strikes in every sector, coupled with an alarming rise in the incidence of armed robbery. Government alienated many supporters when it dealt with striking workers in the public sector with heavy-handed clumsiness, dismissing those who went on strike for more than a 10 per cent increase in salary, in the face of inflation fast approaching ten times that amount. In June 1980 the entire work-force of Ghana Industrial Holdings Corporation (GIHOC) were dismissed for holding rowdy demonstrations in Accra. The GIHOC Workers Union petitioned the High Court for the dismissals to be reversed, but without success. The secretary of the union, Joachim Amartey Kwei, was to seek his own personal revenge in dramatic fashion in 1982.

Workers in the public sector suffered more than most during these years, for the state was literally running out of money and could not pay them proper wages. In some state-owned factories managers attempted to buy off worker discontent by offering allocations of the factory's products to supplement inadequate wages. Workers, who were expected to sell these goods above controlled prices on the unofficial market, were thus drawn into a web of corruption which further undermined their moral fibre. The fact that workers benefited from this system, in however small a way, may account in part for the initial lack of worker enthusiasm for the revolution when it came on 31 December 1981.

Good ideas were indeed being developed by certain ministers in the Limann administration, but few practical results emerged in those first two years. There appeared to be an attitude in government that now the perceived 'threat' from the military had been 'dealt with' by the security services, the country was embarking upon a long and stable era of civilian administration and thus the present government had many years in which to sort out the country's problems. There was no sense of urgency: no sign of the sort of highly visible crisis management which might have restored a semblance of credibility to the system. On one shocking occasion in July 1980 Parliament could not even raise a quorum of fifty members for the conduct of the business of the House. It appeared to the functionaries of the PNP, both inside and outside of Parliament, that the only likely source of opposition to their continued rule was a weak and divided parliamentary opposition. They were blind to the realities outside their own front door.

While there may well have been a majority of straight and honest individual ministers, there was also a lot of profligate government spending and many dubious deals centred around the importation of consumer goods. The PFP parliamentary leader, Mr S.A.Odoi-Sykes identified the root of the problem in February 1981 when he accused leading members of the PNP, and their unelected functionaries, of being more concerned with the next election than solving the country's problems. He accused them of amassing wealth for themselves and their party through the allocation of import licences, the sale of essential commodities above approved prices and the award of contracts and tenders to friends of the PNP. The sort of thing he was referring to was the importation of two million cutlasses and fishing nets from China which farmers and fishermen rejected as unsuitable. It was government money wasted, but someone made a lot of money on the deal. In May 1981 the Ministry of Agriculture was forced to admit having 'lost' thirteen imported tractors intended for the farmers of Ashanti Region, while the following month Mr Odoi-Sykes revealed that the Ghana National Procurement Agency (GNPA) had 'lost' $1.3 million worth of imported rice, milk and sugar over the previous twelve months. The rice contracts, it was confirmed, had been awarded to friends of the PNP.

On the second anniversary of his administration Limann

admitted that the success of his government's efforts was being jeopardised by the malpractices of over-invoicing, under-invoicing, short-loading of goods and evasion of taxes. 'Unless we change our old habits,' Limann prophetically warned, 'we shall fail to achieve our objectives and may even end up in a national disaster again!' But Limann had little new to offer for the next two years beyond promising that agriculture would continue to be 'the priority area' and that more money would be spent on roads and bridges.

The reality was that the 1981 cocoa harvest was 'locked up' in the rural areas for want of vehicles and passable roads to convey it to the ports. A deal between the army and the Cocoa Marketing Board (CMB) to evacuate the cocoa had recently broken down and the cocoa harvest meanwhile was rotting in the farmers' inadequate storage houses. The same applied to other crops, so that Limann's long-overdue announcement on 6 November 1981 of large increases in prices paid per bag for cocoa, coffee and shea-nut, meant little to the farmers who could not get their crops to market.

The continued ineffectiveness of the PNP government aroused considerable frustration in the country at large. Within the PNP itself, the left-wing intellectuals of the Youth Wing felt betrayed by the party which had used the name of Nkrumah to get itself elected. Out of that same sense of disillusionment emerged the Kwame Nkrumah Revolutionary Guard (KNRG), but their last-ditch efforts to salvage the ideological integrity of the party were ultimately doomed to failure. The parliamentary opposition, anticipating the imminent collapse of the PNP's majority, began to make moves towards the unification of the minority parties in Parliament. But in the event they never got the chance to test the effectiveness of their new alignment for the initiative was already moving into the hands of those who were opposed to the whole concept of parliamentary opposition.

During 1980 and 1981 opposition to the PNP government had begun to coalesce around a number of left-wing groups which were operating outside the parliamentary process. The most radical of these were the June Fourth Movement (JFM) and the New Democratic Movement (NDM), both of them founded by small groups of students and academic intellectuals who, through the late 1970s, had developed a Marxist-oriented interpretation of the Ghanaian situation. Both groups had drawn much of their impetus from the AFRC period and it was only following the handover of 24 September that they became formal organisations.

The JFM, as its name implies, had as its initial inspiration, the aim of upholding the gains of the June 4th Revolution and after Rawlings' enforced retirement from the Air Force, it was able to draw him into the movement. Rawlings, as already mentioned, traced his links with radical students back to the mid-1970s when he was looking for ways to overthrow the Acheampong regime. He had been impressed by their defiant stand against the UNIGOV concept and he had had frequent meetings with radical students during the AFRC period. More often than not, on those occasions he was attempting to cool their demands for more blood while at the same time not wishing to dampen their inspirational revolutionary fervour.

Rawlings was drawn to the socialist and anti-imperialist rhetoric of the JFM's founding members, but his acceptance of the chairmanship of the organisation in early 1980 should not lead one to conclude that he had become an intellectually committed socialist like his colleagues in the JFM. He shared many of their ideals, but later history was to reveal the extent of his intellectual distance from them when it came to the practicalities of running a revolution. Rawlings remained an immensely practical man. His prime concern was for the poor and the exploited and he riled at the injustice and moral decadence of the country's ruling élite.

From the JFM's point of view, Rawlings was an ideal leader of the movement, for his high profile representation of the June Fourth concept brought the movement into an immediate prominence which might otherwise have eluded it. Above all, of course, Rawlings represented the means by which a revolution might be staged. His forced retirement from the Air Force notwithstanding, his leadership of the JFM brought into the organisation a number of useful radical soldiers, especially from among the non-commissioned ranks.

The JFM, NDM and other left-wing movements of the period were important in providing the ideological rationale for the 31 December revolution of 1981, as well as providing a corps of dedicated cadres who could implement a revolutionary programme on a national scale and thus hopefully avoid a lot of the chaotic lack of direction which had characterised the AFRC experience. In the meantime, the JFM in particular provided Rawlings with a public platform from which to 'sensitise' the people and to hold the government to account.

On the occasion of the first anniversary of the June 4th Revolution, Rawlings warned: 'We will not look on while the people continue to suffer.' A year later he had moved on apace. In a press conference to commemorate the second anniversary of the revolution his attitude had become: 'those who make a peaceful revolution impossible make a violent revolution inevitable.'

By then some people in the rural areas had been refusing to enter their names on the voting register on the grounds that they had been fooled by parliamentary politicians for far too long. Promises made at election time were not being fulfilled and, according to one report, life in the villages was becoming 'almost unbearable'. Rawlings picked up their theme and revealed the maturing of his political ideology when he referred to 'the gigantic struggle not only for political democracy but also for economic democracy and social justice'. He went on to forecast: 'That struggle will not be won on the pages of a constitutional document.'

Just at a time when Limann's government most needed to regain credibility, the PNP bosses behind the scenes began to pull their party apart in internecine quarrels over control of party policy in the build-up to the next election. In November 1981 a member of the PNP's National Executive Committee, Samuel Addae-Amoako issued a writ in the Accra High Court to restrain the party hierarchy, Chairman Nana Okutwer Bekoe III, General Secretary Dr Ivan Addae-Mensah and Publicity Chairman Kofi Batsa, from rail-roading through party policy in advance of the party's annual congress. The case was settled out of court, but the above three officers of the PNP were ordered to account to the Treasurer within twenty-one days for all monies they had received on behalf of the party. This followed hot on the revelation that a senior member of the PNP had received a commission worth £2.7 million sterling on a currency printing contract in Britain that was going to cost the Ghanaian government a total of £22 million.

As a powerless Dr Limann was prompted to remark: 'All of us have to be judged by our performances and integrity.'

Colonel Bernasko of the Action Congress Party described the government of the day as: 'like a ship without a radar and of which the captain has lost control.'

On Wednesday 30 December 1981 Addae-Amoako revealed to a small group of newsmen that he had been made the PNP's acting national organiser, assigned to pull the party out of the morass of corruption, greed and dictatorship into which it had been dragged by 'a few who think they own the party' and so help the PNP to win the next election. But by then it was already far too late. Within twenty-four hours the military had intervened, the constitution had been suspended and all political parties were proscribed.

Chapter 4

The 31 December Revolution

The coup which launched the 31 December revolution had none of the violence and drama of its counterpart in 1979. The first that most people knew of it was a radio broadcast by Jerry Rawlings at 11.00 a.m. on the morning of Thursday 31 December 1981.

Groups within the military had been expecting it for some time. There were several left-wing coup plots emerging during the early weeks of December and most looked to Rawlings as their leader. Their plans were given added impetus by the knowledge that there was at least one right-wing group within the military who were plotting their own coup with the backing of the hierarchy of the PNP. Military Intelligence moved against the suspected left-wing plotters and their numerous arrests, detention and alleged torture of soldiers or former soldiers associated with the AFRC period in fact helped to precipitate the coup itself.

This time Rawlings wanted to be sure of retaining control of the ranks from the beginning. It was not a mutiny against the officer corps and so the whole thing was achieved in a relatively orderly fashion. When the move came, soon after dawn on the morning of 31 December 1981, the military side of it was over very quickly with very little shooting. The civilian politicians were caught completely unawares. Several of the PNP were arrested at an end-of-year party while others were out of the capital in their rural constituencies for the New Year weekend. Broadcasting

House was seized by 10.00 a.m. and Rawlings came on the air an hour later to declare what he called a 'Holy War' against the 'enemies of the people':

> Fellow Ghanaians, as you will notice, we are not playing the national anthem. In other words, this is not a coup. I ask for *nothing less than a REVOLUTION* – something that will transform the social and economic order of this country.
>
> Fellow citizens, it is now left to you to decide how this country is going to go from today. We are asking for nothing more than popular democracy. We are asking for nothing more than the power to organise this country in such a way that nothing will be done from the Castle without the consent and authority of the people. In other words, the people, the farmers, the police, the soldiers, the workers – you, the guardians – rich or poor, should be a part of the decision-making process of this country.

This would be achieved through the setting up of people's defence committees in the work-places and in every district and village. Decisions, he said, would no longer be left in the hands of those whom he referred to as 'that pack of criminals in the PNP'. The Limann administration had come to an end and all former ministers were to surrender themselves to the police or military authorities. He urged the soldiers to maintain strict military discipline at all times and to refrain from 'barbaric acts', especially looting. He warned, in particular, that nobody should harm the person of Dr Limann who was still at large. Finally, the link with the AFRC period was clearly established when he announced the reinstatement of Brigadier Nunoo-Mensah as Chief of Defence Staff and Brigadier Arnold Quainoo as Army Commander.

The streets and markets of Accra were immediately

deserted as people packed up their wares, closed their offices and went home for the holiday weekend. New Year celebrations carried on that night much as usual though in a slightly subdued fashion. By Saturday morning, 2 January 1982, shops and markets were beginning to reopen. That night Rawlings made a second, lengthier broadcast on radio and television in which he set out in more detail the purpose and direction of the 31 December revolution:

> Good evening, fellow countrymen. To attempt to justify the actions of 31 December 1981 would presuppose that we Ghanaians do not know and feel what has been going on since 24 September 1979. Briefly, it has been nothing short of a clear denial of our fundamental rights as a people to enjoy the wealth of our labour.

He accused the PNP of deliberately reneging on their pledge to continue the 'house-cleaning' exercise and then, in words which were to remain fixed in people's minds for many years to come, he launched into an impassioned and histrionic condemnation of the PNP's record in office:

> This has been the most disgraceful government in the history of this country. It is only in recent times that criminals and such like have become respectable in our society ... They have turned our hospitals into graveyards and our clinics into death transit camps where men, women and children die daily because of lack of drugs and basic equipment.

Rawlings went on to announce the suspension of the Third Republic Constitution of 1979, the dismissal of all members of the government, the dissolution of Parliament and the banning of all political parties. Power had been assumed by the Provisional National Defence Council (PNDC), the members of whom would be announced later.

He then explained his understanding of the kind of real democracy that he wanted to see emerge in Ghana:

> To many of us, if not all of us, democracy does not just mean paper guarantees of abstract liberties. It involves, above all, food, clothing and shelter, in the absence of which life is not worth living.
>
> Fellow countrymen, the time has now come for us to restructure this society in a real and meaningful democratic manner so as to ensure the involvement and *active participation of the people in the decision-making process.*

This last phrase was to become an oft-repeated guiding principle upon which any sensible assessment of the 31 December revolution should be assessed.

Over the next few days the President, Dr Limann, was detained and the remaining ministers were arrested, some of them trying to flee the country. The PNP's chairman, Nana Okutwer Bekoe tried to slip across the border at Kute in Volta Region, dressed in the ragged clothing of a poor peasant; but he was unable to hide his ample girth, more characteristic of a prosperous businessman than a lean and hungry peasant! The suspicions of an alert border guard were immediately aroused and he was promptly arrested.

The coup of 31 December 1981 initially lacked the immediate popular acclaim which had greeted Ghana's previous coups. It caught most people unawares. New Year's Eve was an important social and religious festival, starting with church services and moving on to celebrations in people's homes and on the streets. On the morning of 31 December most people were engaged in preparations for the festival and politics was the last thing on their minds. Many were unsure how to react and some felt uneasy that the coup had interrupted a religious festival.

In general the first reaction was: 'Oh no, not again!'

The view of the business and professional classes, who made up the bulk of the party politicians, was of course wholly pessimistic. For them it was a very worrying time. They recalled only too well the unconstitutional acts and revolutionary tendencies of the AFRC period. They had largely supported the attempts to reverse the decisions of the AFRC's Special Courts and they had generally gone along with the idea that the main source of instability for a civilian administration was ambitious individuals in the military rather than poverty and bad government. Now here were these same June 4th revolutionaries, come back to haunt them! On the face of it, the prosperous bourgeoisie had much to lose from a revolutionary government that claimed to want to restructure Ghanaian society in the interests of the illiterate masses.

After an initial two weeks of remaining quiet and hoping to avoid arrest, the professional classes, through their Association of Recognised Professional Bodies, called on the PNDC to re-enact the human rights provisions of the Third Republic Constitution to ensure the liberties of the individual were preserved. It is interesting to note their continued caution at this stage, for although they reaffirmed their faith in constitutional government and said that the military should not have intervened, they admitted the failures of the PNP administration. They did not call for the immediate reinstatement of civilian rule, but merely urged a handover at the end of the Limann term, in 1983.

One of the earliest public demonstrations of feeling about the coup was a gathering of protest in the Upper Region capital of Bolgatanga. The people there identified Rawlings' return to power as a deliberate military move against a northern President. In due course, however, they were somewhat reassured by the presence of a number of northern faces in the new administration.

It took a few days for support for the coup to emerge from the workers in whose name the 'Holy War' had been declared and in this respect the June Fourth Movement was crucial in providing the link between the military who had staged the coup and the civilians who would turn it into a revolution. In due course they were joined by cadres from the New Democratic Movement, the People's Revolutionary League, the African Youth Command and the PNP's own Kwame Nkrumah Revolutionary Guard, all of whom helped over the next few months to mobilise support for the nascent revolution. In response to Rawlings' second broadcast, some 2000 workers gathered in Accra on Sunday 3 January to listen to an address by Mr Kwesi Adu and others of the June Fourth Movement. They carried placards proclaiming 'Death to Kalabule' and 'We support the PNDC', but theirs was at this stage more a demonstration against the PNP than a vote of confidence in the new government which had yet to reveal its policies. So far, the workers appear simply to have felt an instinctive trust for Rawlings' integrity, and there was no doubt about his general popularity.

On Tuesday 5 January Rawlings returned once again to Broadcasting House to explain in greater depth what the revolution was all about. It was, he explained, an 'opening for real democracy' for all Ghanaian people: soldiers and civilians. The only people who might oppose it were those rich businessmen and comfortable bureaucrats who, since 24 September 1979, had been doing very well at the expense of the 'toiling and sweating' masses. The tools to implement the new revolutionary democracy were the local Defence Committees to which he had referred in his first broadcast. People must set these up themselves 'at all levels of our national life, in the towns, in the villages, in all our factories, offices and work-places and in the barracks'. Their role was to defend the revolution, expose 'saboteurs', confront unjust employers and thwart corrupt private deals by businessmen and managers which raised the prices of goods for the poor consumers. At the same time, People's Tribunals would be set up to investigate 'crimes against the people', in particular, corruption and abuse of office. Unlike the AFRC's controversial Special Courts, these Tribunals would be public and would be seen to be fair. They would operate parallel to the traditional judicial system which would still remain in place, but, unlike the traditional courts, the Tribunals would not be 'fettered in their procedures by technical rules which in the past have perverted the course of justice and enabled criminals to go free' – a direct reference to the freeing of AFRC convicts during the Limann administration.

By the time of Rawlings' third broadcast the message was getting through to the mass of the people that this was indeed *their* revolution. Over the next few days numerous demonstrations took place in Accra and other cities in support of the PNDC. On Friday 8 January the traffic of the capital was brought to a halt as residents witnessed the biggest gathering in the city in recent history. Tens of thousands of workers came in from all over the Accra-Tema metropolitan area and crowded towards Nicholson Stadium, Burma Camp to hear Rawlings speak. Their placards proclaimed with millenial fervour: 'We have embraced the Holy War', 'JJ our Moses', 'Arise Rawlings for Limann wants to destroy your children'. And in response to Rawlings' appeal, in the days and weeks that followed, Workers' Defence Committees began to be formed in state corporations, factories and offices.

Apart from building popular support to legitimise its seizure of power, the immediate practical task of the new government was to evacuate the cocoa harvest, the coffee and the foodstuffs which had become 'locked up' in the rural areas for want of proper transport, decent roads and energetic leadership. Colonel W.M.Mensah-Wood, Commander of the Field Engineers' Regiment, was appointed to head an emergency task force, and to provide volunteers for the work, the three universities and other colleges of higher education were closed until April. The students set to with enthusiasm and over the next six weeks hundreds of thousands of bags of cocoa were successfully evacuated to the port of Tema, much to the surprise of world market dealers based in London who had raised the price of cocoa by £75 a ton on the assumption that the new revolutionary government in Ghana would fail to get its crop to market. The success of the student task force, which was engaged in many other rural rehabilitation tasks as well, gained the new regime a lot of credibility and support in its first few crucial months in office.

On Monday 11 January a decree was published formally setting out the structure and powers of the PNDC. The Council assumed all the executive powers of government. Rawlings was Chairman and the other members were Brigadier Nunoo-Mensah, the Chief of Defence Staff; Reverend Dr Vincent Kwabina Damuah, a Catholic priest with a strong record of service among the poor; Warrant Officer Joseph Adjei Buadi, Co-ordinator of the Armed Forces' Defence Committees; Sergeant Alolga Akata-Pore, an active member of the left-wing Movement on National Affairs (MONAS) and a recent student of economics at the University of Cape Coast; Joachim Amartey Kwei, former secretary-general of the GIHOC Workers' Union and the only civilian to have been actively involved in the coup; and Chris Bukari Atim, secretary of the June Fourth Movement. The decree allowed for the appointment of further members to the Council, up to a maximum of eleven. In addition a National Defence Committee was established to advise the Council. The Electoral Commission, which hitherto had been concerned with the registration of voters and the conduct of elections was to be transformed into a National Commission for Democracy whose role was to safeguard the democratic process by seeing that central government satisfied the needs of the people.

It was this issue of a new form of people's democracy that the PNDC's revolution was most concerned to implement. It was, after all, the perceived failure of the Third Republic's form of democratic government that had provided Rawlings and his colleagues with the justification for seizing power in the name of establishing a people's government. An understanding of the political philosophy of the PNDC, at the time it came to power, is therefore crucial to an understanding of the revolution itself and the way that it developed.

The political philosophy of the PNDC was strongly influenced by the model of revolutionary socialism espoused by the former student leaders and radical intellectuals of the June Fourth Movement, in particular, Nicholas Atampugri, Kwesi Adu, Chris Atim, Nyeya Yen and Sergeant Alolga Akata-Pore. People such as these articulated socialist rhetoric which they used to try to convince Rawlings that in their ideas he had the basis for a people's revolution.

The JFM's view of socialism was inspired in the first place by what they saw as the gains of the June 4th Revolution. The mutiny of the ranks in the armed forces in 1979 had shown the way. For once the ordinary downtrodden commoner had stood up and defied his exploiters. Not very much in practical terms had been achieved in those few months. The gains were primarily psychological. The common people had gained in self-respect and the principle had been firmly established in the minds of the people that the country's rulers were ultimately answerable to them, in whose name they ruled.

Building upon this inspiration, the JFM proposed that the way to achieve effective people's democracy was to establish 'defence committees' along the lines of the Libyan and Cuban models. Captain Kojo Tsikata had already convinced Rawlings of the value of defence committees. According to this model, people would gather together at their place of work, residential community or village and elect an executive committee who would safeguard their interests and organise the people for whatever task was needed. In the work-place they would in effect be factory-floor trades unions, and would thus supplant to some extent the Trade Union Congress (TUC) which, in the view of the JFM and PNDC, had become bureaucratic and divorced from the interests of the workers. The new Workers' Defence Committees (WDCs) would monitor the management of their factories and work-places, watch out for corruption in the handling and invoicing of raw materials and finished products and generally become involved in the day-to-day 'decision-making process' of the company.

Similarly, in the residential townships of the cities and in the villages of the rural areas, People's Defence Committees (PDCs), with their locally-elected executive committees, would safeguard the day-to-day interests of the local people, protect tenants from unjust landlords and see that local government services were provided as required. In addition, in the rural areas the PDCs were expected to organise volunteer communal labour as and when required. In this respect they may have drawn some inspiration from the example of the student task force.

This model saw the 'defence committee' as a combination of industrial democracy and community watchdog. It was believed this would provide the mass of common people with far greater participation in the things which affected their daily lives. Hitherto, from their point of view, the remote 'bourgeois' model of parliamentary democracy entailed little more than the casting of a single vote every four or five years and then leaving the running of the country to the propertied, professional and managerial class who had been shown to be primarily concerned with pursuing their own interests. Such was the theory. The practice was somewhat different.

To co-ordinate the activities of the defence committees and provide a link with central government, an Interim National Co-ordinating Committee (INCC) was established. It drew its personnel from both the June Fourth Movement and the New Democratic Movement and in this lay the seeds of ideological conflict. The NDM, which had held aloof from the notion of staging an actual coup, regarded the 31 December revolution as premature and the JFM as a 'bunch of adventurers'. The ideological conflict between the JFM and the NDM within the INCC prevented the development of the kind of clear direction from the centre that was so badly needed. As a result, the defence committee concept was not properly structured or led from the beginning. It depended too much on goodwill and local initiative. Each defence committee had its own concept of the revolution and its own agenda.

The initial guidelines for the defence committees had specifically excluded the middle classes. It was a serious error of judgement which stemmed from a simplistic division of the population into 'citizens' and 'people'. The revolution was for 'the people'. 'Citizens' – those with property or other forms of visible wealth – were by definition 'enemies of the revolution'. It led to much arbitrary verbal and physical abuse as the managerial class, the businessmen and the professionals, who had been running the country, became unnecessarily alienated from the revolution. In the work-places, WDCs ousted managers from their offices and took over factories with no idea how to manage them. Industrial production, already far below capacity, plummeted to new depths. In the residential and rural areas, many of the PDCs attracted to themselves the unemployed and the unemployable, the 'bully-boys' of the local community, who carried through private conflicts and pursued personal vendettas. It was enough for someone to be identified as 'an enemy of the revolution' to justify a severe assault.

Within a matter of weeks, power to the people became power to the brutal and the violent in society, especially those with guns. Arbitrary assaults and even killings were carried out in the name of the revolution, many of them by armed police, border guards and soldiers. The *Graphic* and the *Times* reported the frequent exhortations of Regional Secretaries and Council members who urged defence committees to refrain from brutalities and arbitrary acts of violence; they were supposed to be acting in the interests of the oppressed, not as the oppressors themselves. There were, however, significantly few public condemnations of the conduct of the armed forces who seem to have been responsible for most of the killings. Although the frequent condemnation of these brutalities was given wide publicity, very few of the actual incidents being condemned were ever reported in the media. To some extent this was deliberate policy on the part of the state-owned papers: a tactical desire to play down the dark side of the revolutionary process. In many cases, however, reporters were too scared to make the necessary investigations and when they did arrive on the scene of a reported incident, they could seldom find anyone prepared to come forward as a witness.

At the end of July 1982 the Association of Recognised Professional Bodies (ARPB) published a list of 180 named victims of murder since 31 December 1981 in which no prosecution had taken place, or seemed likely to take place. The ARPB's bold action was prompted by a particularly shocking multiple killing. Many of the victims named in their list were known to have been shot by trigger-happy military personnel who used the loaded gun as a means of enforcing their own arbitrary orders. The ARPB's bulletin provoked angry reaction from certain quarters and two meeting halls used by members of the ARPB were ransacked by an unruly mob. Significantly the PNDC failed to issue any public condemnation of these latest acts of vandalism, a point which merely served to convince many people that they had been conducted at the behest of the government.

That first year of PNDC rule saw the assertion of naked power and a settling of old scores by resort to violence; and however much Rawlings and the members of his government condemned these 'excesses of the revolution' as undermining the positive aspects of the process, they, as leaders of that revolution must bear some of the responsibility for acts committed in its name.

The darkest point in all those dark days was the killing of three High Court judges and a retired army major on the night of 30 June 1982. Justices F.P.Sarkodee, K.A.Agyepong and Cecilia Koranteng Addow, all of whom had been prominent in overturning the decisions of the AFRC's Special Courts, and Major Sam Acquah, Director of Personnel at Ghana Industrial Holding Corporation (GIHOC), were seized from their homes under cover of darkness and taken to a military firing range on the Accra plains. There, gathered together under a tree, they were shot dead and their bodies partly burned in an unsuccessful attempt to cover up the deed.

At first it was thought the victims were being held by kidnappers, and Johnny Hansen, Secretary for the Interior, describing the seizure of the judges as 'unprecedented in the history of Ghana', reported that the police were working round the clock to find them. The charred bodies were seen by some military personnel on the morning of Saturday 3 July, but, in what can only be taken as an indication of the frequency with which they saw such sights, they did not report their findings until after they had finished the day's exercise and returned to barracks some eight hours later. By then it was too late to remove the decomposing bodies that night and it was thus Sunday 4 July before the bodies were finally recovered and positively identified.

That night a badly shaken Chairman Rawlings announced on national television the discovery of the four bodies. He expressed horror at 'these hideous acts of terrorism', describing the crime as against all the principles of the revolution. He concluded that it must have been committed by 'enemies of the revolution', who hoped by this dastardly act to plunge the nation into anarchy and chaos.

In the days that followed, workers' groups, students' organisations and Secretaries of State all condemned the murders in forthright terms. One caught the mood when he described this crime as 'a stain on Ghana's history'. Father Vincent Damuah, however, was one of the few government spokesmen who admitted the possibility of a link between the judges' killings and the large number of other cases of extra-judicial killing and soldiers molesting people. His calls for a full investigation of all cases of violence by the forces of 'law and order' at this particularly sensitive time for the PNDC were seen by some as likely to undermine the government and many were not surprised when he resigned from the Council on 18 August.

A Special Investigations Board was set up on 15 July to investigate the killings, but by then rumours had already begun to circulate which alleged that members of the PNDC itself were involved in the crime and that the killing of these particular judges, who had overturned the rulings of the AFRC, was in fact welcomed by the government, if not actually committed at its instigation. Rumours got to such a pitch that a week later Rawlings himself was driven to protest publicly his innocence and that of other members of the PNDC. He pointed out that such a deed was totally against the interests of the government, particularly at a time when it badly needed to regain public credibility. The fact that the rumours had gained such a hold, however, was an indication of the extent to which the PNDC was losing the confidence of some articulate sections of the community in this matter. What made matters worse was that the rumours were not entirely without foundation.

Over the next five months the Special Investigations Board gradually unravelled the sordid details of the plot. A Lance Corporal and three colleagues confessed to the killing; but most significant of all, it emerged that the whole thing had been organised by Joachim Amartey Kwei, a member of the PNDC until his resignation in August 1982.

Amartey Kwei made his first sworn testimony to the Board in October 1982, and the confession of one of his co-conspirators implicated Alolga Akata-Pore, another member of Council, in part of the plot, although not the actual murder. Finally, in November, in what in retrospect can only be seen as an attempt to blackmail the PNDC into saving him from the firing-squad, Amartey Kwei tried to implicate Captain Kojo Tsikata, Special Security Adviser to the PNDC and close colleague of Chairman Rawlings. Although the Chairman of the Special Investigations Board, Justice Crabbe, accepted this latest allegation and recommended Tsikata's arrest and prosecution, the Attorney-General decided otherwise.

In his review of the Board's findings, the Attorney-General pointed out that Amartey Kwei had made three separate statements of confession before the SIB, each one in some manner contradictory of the others, and it was only in the third confession that he chose to implicate Captain Tsikata. The Attorney-General argued that the inconsistency of the confessions made Amartey Kwei an unreliable witness and, there being no corroborating evidence, there were insufficient grounds to permit a prosecution of Tsikata. Amartey Kwei himself admitted Tsikata's innocence just before his own execution for the murder in August 1983.

It was thus finally concluded that Amartey Kwei had acted on his own initiative, in what he considered to be justifiable action against 'enemies of the revolution'. The inclusion of Major Acquah along with the three judges was clearly an act of personal vengeance for Acquah's role in the dismissal of the GIHOC workers in June 1980.

Notwithstanding the official conclusion, ever since 1982 the murder of judges has, in the words of one prominent member of the government, 'hung like a sword of Damocles' above the head of the PNDC. Rawlings and his inner circle of advisers have been accused by their critics of not acting promptly or strongly enough against the suspected perpetrators of this dastardly crime. Despite the thoroughness of the investigation and the action taken on the SIB's report, they are accused of having been more concerned with the survival of the PNDC than with the pursuit of justice in those critical months of 1982. Indeed, the PNDC is generally so distrusted on this matter that it is believed in some circles that Amartey Kwei was never executed, but was spirited out of the country and is still alive in exile!

In the aftermath of the judges' murders Rawlings and the PNDC began to take firmer action against the 'excesses of the revolution' and before the end of July a Military Tribunal was set up to try soldiers and police who assaulted, molested or unlawfully arrested any person. 'The more you terrorise people,' Rawlings warned the Second Infantry Battalion in Kumasi, 'the more you create enemies.' Since the general mutiny against the senior officer corps in 1979, the military had been badly in need of a thorough reorganisation. General Arnold Quainoo now took on this task. Over the next three years he knocked the army back into shape, restoring discipline and respect for law and order. In fact he was so harsh with cases of indiscipline that he almost provoked a backlash and he certainly lost much of his former popularity.

Although most people, even those within the government, do not seem to have realised it at the time, by July 1982 the revolution had reached a critical turning point in its historical evolution. It was a time of mounting economic crisis, with no clear solution yet in sight. It was a time of internal political crisis, as ideological conflicts within the organs of government threatened to pull the PNDC apart. On top of this came the deteriorating security situation and the general crisis in popular confidence, brought out into the open by the judges' murders.

The Catholic Church, which had begun the revolution with empathy for the underlying principle of grass-roots responsibility and government accountability, had by July become sorely disillusioned. In the view of the Church hierarchy, despite its early good intentions, the revolution had lost its way. Not only did they disapprove of the means, but the ends themselves were not even being achieved. A Catholic bishops' communiqué, issued on 10 July, spoke for many when it said:

> Of late, inhumanities of epidemic proportions have been committed with impunity. Villagers and the marginalised of our society are terrorised and intimidated ... Humble men, women and children have been and are being molested, maimed, killed or otherwise repressed without cause ... The powerless of our nation have been rendered more helpless through the indiscipline and arbitrary action of people who have constituted themselves into demi-gods ... Fear hangs on the head of any successful man like the proverbial sword. The result is that we are losing the cream of our society. To avoid unwarranted disgrace, people are fleeing the country as if it were some deadly pestilence. Ghanaians who do not follow a particular line of thought are branded as the enemies of the people. The injustice is too glaring to escape the attention of even the most casual genuine observer ... In the face of the present moral, legal, political and social disorder, the insidious lack of economic accountability of the past pales into insignificance.

Rawlings knew the moment was critical and that the process he had started on 31 December was in serious danger of derailment. He realised that it was up to him to seize the initiative and use the full powers of his leadership to drag the revolution back on course.

In a major speech to the nation on radio and television on 29 July 1982 Rawlings assessed the state of the revolution after seven months in power. He did not attempt to gloss over the 'certain regrettable incidents involving members of the People's Army and the public', nor the 'cases of harassment of innocent civilians by persons who are expected to protect them'. The PNDC, he protested, had never condoned such incidents in the past and, with the aid of the new military tribunals, it would continue to do everything in its power to bring them under control and punish the guilty.

He then turned to the defence committees, which had come in for so much criticism. Their limitations were in their lack of direction and the abuse of power by certain selfish and misguided individuals. On the positive side, he listed their achievements in the field of exposing corruption, curbing smuggling, clearing refuse and enforcing price controls. He saw their most positive impact in their raising of the level of public political consciousness. 'The introduction of these institutions,' he asserted, 'has arrested the cynical apathy which had gripped this nation.' In order to strengthen these institutions, bring them under greater control and thus safeguard their vital democratic elements, a new National Defence Committee would take over the role of the INCC and co-ordinate the PDCs and WDCs at local, district and regional levels. As part of this rationalisation, the illogical and negative distinction between citizen and people was removed and the middle classes and managers were encouraged to join and be active participants in the defence committee movement.

In a direct reference to the ARPB's call the previous day for a prompt handover to constitutional rule, however, the Chairman continued:

> Certain persons and organisations are asking us to hand over power. From what I have said so far and from the nature of their demands, it would appear that what they really want to do is to take

> power away from the people and hand it over to them.
>
> These persons and organisations are not interested in participating in collective decision-making. What they want is to monopolise power and decision-making. If they are really interested in democratic processes and in the sovereignty of the people, I would advise them to join the people of this country and participate within the framework of the structures we are creating to ensure democratic rule and sovereignty of the people.

It was a clear re-affirmation of his faith in the revolution. It also served notice to those who imagined or hoped that as the nation's problems became increasingly insoluble, the revolution would collapse and Rawlings would be forced to hand over power once again to the professional politicians. To them he said: 'There is no compromise on this issue . . . There is no U-turn!'

Although he laid particular emphasis on the political issues of the revolution, Rawlings knew as well as anybody that it was on the economic front that the 31 December revolution would ultimately stand or fall. There was no doubt that at that critical moment in the second half of 1982, the nation's economic problems were almost insurmountable and a major part of his speech that 29 July was devoted to the economic crisis. In this Rawlings was laying the foundations for the tough economic decisions that he knew lay ahead.

The economy that the PNDC inherited on 31 December 1981 was in a state approaching bankruptcy. There is little doubt, however, as critics of the PNDC are quick to point out, that, barring the remarkably successful evacuation of the cocoa harvest, the revolution itself was responsible for an even greater deterioration in the state of the economy. The anti-imperialist rhetoric of the PNDC meant that many aid arrangements which the Limann administration had in the pipeline were temporarily suspended as Western capitalists and bankers hesitated to risk their capital in such a volatile situation. At the same time the early months of near anarchy in the country meant that industrial and agricultural production were driven ever further into decline. Even so, the balance sheet that faced the PNDC at the beginning of 1982 was an unenviable one for any government.

Disposable foreign exchange at the end of 1981 consisted of $33 million, barely sufficient to cover two weeks of imports. Outstanding short-term commitments, needed to pay for goods already imported, stood at $348 million, and there was hardly any commercial bank abroad which would confirm letters of credit for any of Ghana's local banks. At the same time, the Ghana National Procurement Agency and the Food Distribution Corporation had between them enough maize for just ten days' consumption and enough rice to last for three months. The supply of drugs to the health service and raw materials to industry were in an even worse state. Added to this, the rise in world oil prices in 1980 – 81 meant that in the first six months of 1982 Ghana was forced to spend $100 million, three-quarters of all her precious foreign exchange, on crude oil imports.

One of the first things the PNDC did on assuming office was to set up an Economic Review Committee to assess the true extent of the crisis and make proposals for its solution. Two key members of the Review Committee were Dr J.L.S. Abbey, who had been Commissioner for Finance under Akuffo and had advised the AFRC, and Dr Kwesi Botchwey, a lecturer at the University of Ghana. The latter was well-known for his radical, anti-imperialist stance. He was recommended to the PNDC by the left-wing intellectuals of the June Fourth Movement, and it was assumed by them that he would uphold their cause.

The socialist formula of the JFM, that influenced the PNDC's policy-making in the initial stages of the revolution, consisted of three basic ingredients: firstly, to deal with corruption in business management, state corporations, banking, civil service and personal taxation; secondly, to redistribute power, and hence wealth, to the people; and thirdly, to solicit aid from fellow-revolutionaries and major socialist countries. A Citizen's Vetting Committee was set up to flush out the first, the defence committees were designed to deal with the second, and delegations were sent abroad to seek the third.

The first major aid-seeking delegation went to Libya towards the end of February. It was led by Chris Atim, a prominent ideologue of the JFM who had been active during the previous weeks in inaugurating defence committees in the cities and rural areas. Libya had already donated a plane-load of rice, flour and milk to the people of Ghana in the second week of the revolution. Atim now came back with promises of more aid and a consignment of newsprint for the *Graphic* and the *Mirror*. Libya's main contribution to Ghana's revolution was a consignment of 28 000 metric tons of crude oil in July: the first of twelve such consignments over the next six months, each on free credit for a year and interest-free repayment after that. Although this was the sum total of Libya's aid, it was of major importance to the survival of Ghana at this particularly critical time.

In April Atim led another delegation abroad in search of financial support from some of the 'progressive nations of the world'. His team visited Cuba, Eastern Europe and the Soviet Union, but came back with little more than expressions of socialist solidarity. The Soviet Union in particular had had its fingers burned in Ghana in 1966 and it was not prepared to risk its capital again just on the say-so that the PNDC was 'revolutionary'.

The only other sources of the kind of outside finance which Ghana so desperately needed to survive, let alone to recover, were the banking and donor agencies of the capitalist world of Western Europe and North America; and the only way to get access to their funds was through the backing of the International Monetary Fund (IMF) and the World Bank. Such a route, however, was anathema to the socialist ideologues of the PNDC and, in particular, the June Fourth Movement. To them, the IMF spelt imperialist intervention in Third World affairs. They held up the example of Zaïre as an African country with a long history of IMF support and pointed to the disastrous situation that pertained in that country and to the lack of benefits for its people. What they failed to take into consideration, however, was the extent of corruption at the highest level in Zaïre and that the surplus revenue derived from the Zaïrean people's efforts was being stashed abroad in numbered bank accounts. Ghana's case was very different. Here was a revolutionary government, which held accountability to the people as a primary guiding principle. It did not follow, therefore, that support from the IMF need necessarily be a negative experience. There remained, however, one major stumbling block, and it was called 'devaluation'.

It was well-known that when the IMF drew up or approved a rescue package for a beleaguered Third World economy, one of the basic requirements they insisted on was a thorough re-evaluation of the currency, to bring it closer into line with world market rates. In the majority of cases, for the Third World country involved, this meant devaluation.

The sort of country which needed to turn to the IMF for support had usually been subsidising its currency for many years in order to protect its weak economy and its underpaid population from the full rigours of competing on equal terms with the powerful, capitalist nations of the world. By over-valuing their currency, governments ensured that imports of foreign consumer goods – usually manufactured items, but sometimes basic foodstuffs – were relatively cheap and at a price that the population could afford. The other side of an over-valued currency, however, was that the price received for exports was also artificially low. Thus the cocoa farmer, the timber merchant and the gold-mining company would receive in local currency only a fraction of what their produce was really worth abroad. The most extreme example in Ghana's case had been in 1975–77 when the world price for cocoa had soared to a record level of £3000 a ton. Endemic corruption aside, the Cocoa Marketing Board of Ghana, dependent on an artificially over-valued currency, received very little benefit from this, and the cocoa farmer even less.

On the other hand, to accept devaluation, as a means of gaining access to the world market, looked very much like bowing to the dictates of Western neo-colonialism, which controlled world market prices, largely to its own benefit. It was a prospect against which Nkrumah had so eloquently warned back in 1965. Yet, even Nkrumah had been obliged to face the realities of world trade and entered negotiations with the IMF in 1965.

In Ghana's case, in 1982, what was the alternative? Socialist aid was amounting to very little, and certainly not enough for the country's recovery needs. Whatever happened, Ghana must export in order to be able to import the consumer goods she needed; and that meant dealing with the capitalist world market. The only way to escape the neo-colonial stranglehold was to confront it straight on: strengthen the basis of one's own economy, build on one's natural advantages and the resourcefulness of the people and so, eventually, be able to compete aggressively with the most powerful economies in the world. A number of emerging countries in eastern Asia had shown that it was possible, even if at considerable social cost. Why not in Africa too?

These were the issues that exercised the minds of the Economic Review Committee during the first half of 1982. For years the Ghanaian economy had suffered from irresponsible fiscal management. The important issue now, apart from balancing government finances and getting out of recurrent debt, was to shift the emphasis of economic policy away from the rhetoric of redistribution and concentrate instead on an increase in industrial and agricultural production. Fundamental, however, to any serious restructuring of the economy, was devaluation, so that those who *were* producing for the market could be paid the real value for their products, without a massive subsidy from government, which ultimately either drew its money from greater foreign debt or from the pockets of the people. If the Ghanaian team came up with a package of proposals which showed a firm commitment to stabilising the budget and readjusting the exchange rate, then it would be able to go the International Monetary Fund for the necessary financial backing.

Some work had already been done with personnel from the Fund in 1978/79 and again in 1981. The godfathers of the PNP who controlled the Limann administration, however, had not been prepared to take the political risk of devaluation. When the Fund offered to come back in 1982, the Ghanaian Review Committee told them to wait: they would do their own assessment and approach the Fund, in due course, with their own set of proposals. By August 1982 the Review Committee had assembled a preliminary package of proposals. The World Bank and IMF annual meetings were coming up and they realised that before they proceeded any further they needed the firm political backing of the whole government. A full meeting of the PNDC, the Committee of Secretaries and the National Defence Council was called to discuss the proposals.

Rawlings was briefed before the meeting and he understood and accepted the arguments for a shift of emphasis towards production and a devaluation of the currency in order to reward the producers. As he put it so succinctly, 'You cannot redistribute poverty.' Dr Kwesi Botchwey, Chairman of the Review Committee and Secretary for Finance, was absent from the country at the time and it was left to Dr Joe Abbey to present the proposals to the meeting.

Abbey explained that at present in Ghana it did not make sense for anybody to produce for export, because they got paid very little for their efforts. This led to a scarcity of foreign exchange, which in turn encouraged people to resort to smuggling. The meeting appeared to appreciate the problem and supported Abbey's argument with examples of things such as salt from the coast and sawn timber from Ashanti. Both of these items had for years been important exports to Burkina Faso; but what the producers were getting for them now in foreign exchange, once turned into cedis at the official rate, would not even pay for the transport to Ouagadougou. Importing, on the other hand, was good business in Ghana because foreign exchange was so cheap. Hence the tendency towards corruption in the issuing of import licences. Clearly, the producers needed some kind of bonus payment and the fairest and most sensible way to do this was to surcharge the importers.

So far, the discussion had been amicable, but at this point somebody asked what the difference was between the surcharging proposal and devaluation. Joe Abbey, in what he later realised was perhaps a tactical error, replied, 'It is a matter of semantics.'

Immediately, there was uproar in the meeting chamber and any further prospect of reasoned argument went out the window. The cadres of the NDM were prepared to consider some limited amount of devaluation; but the far left, of whom the JFM cadres were the most vocal, felt they had been misled and betrayed. This was devaluation by the back door, a sell-out to the neo-colonial dictates of the IMF!

Rawlings made his own feelings clear and as the meeting broke up in disarray, the murmurings began in certain circles of the left that Rawlings was attempting to betray the fundamental socialist principles of the revolution. Over the next two months the debate continued, in the press and in many private meetings, but the issue was no longer how to stabilise the economy and solve the country's financial crisis; rather, it was whether devaluation was a betrayal of revolutionary ideology. By October it was becoming clear that the unity which had so far held the disparate elements of the revolution together, had been rent asunder.

The left of the JFM, led by Chris Atim and Alolga Akata-Pore, decided that the only way to get the revolution back on what they saw as the correct course was to get rid of Rawlings. They interpreted his support for the devaluation package as a clear shift to the political right. Either that or his revolutionary rhetoric of 1981 and early 1982 had been nothing but a front to disguise his own real agenda: a populist dictatorship, in hock to Western capital, with himself in permanent power.

The conspiracy evolved because the conspirators believed they had the power to remove Rawlings: Akata-Pore controlled the armed forces' defence committees, Nicholas Atampogri the police defence committees and Atim and others on the NDC the civilian defence committees. The AFRC period having seriously undermined the authority of the senior officer corps, the conspirators, between them, appeared to hold in their hands the main sources of power in the country. The apparent perfect basis for a successful coup was foiled by two crucial factors: the amateurish organisation of the conspirators and the immense popularity of Rawlings among the rank and file.

Akata-Pore was supposed to take over the armed forces, an announcement would be made on the radio that Rawlings had been overthrown, and Chris Atim and the other civilian conspirators would bring the PDCs out onto the streets in a show of massive public support for the coup. As always happens with attempted coups against the PNDC, however, Rawlings' personal popularity among the military rank and file led certain people to leak news of the conspiracy to the authorities. Thus, when Akata-Pore assembled his men in front of Gondar Barracks on the night of Thursday 28 October, they were confronted by an equal number of Rawlings' supporters under the command of Captain Courage Quashigah. Realising he had lost the element of surprise, Akata-Pore abandoned the coup and made strenuous efforts to patch things up with Rawlings. There followed a moment of farce as the civilian conspirators, not realising that the coup had already been cancelled, announced at a special public forum in Accra that Rawlings had been overthrown, a point which Rawlings was easily able to disprove by appearing in public to stress that news of his overthrow was nothing but a silly rumour put about by enemies of the revolution.

In their conspiracy of 28/29 October, the left had shown its hand. Rawlings, however, displayed that element of cool logic which he had developed since the fiery days of 1979 and, for the moment, he chose to play the matter down. This may have been partly because some, such as Atim, had for so long been close personal friends and colleagues; but, perhaps more importantly, the moment was not right. The conspirators had indeed been correct in their assessment of their potential strength in the defence committees. The PDCs, both civilian and military, had proved themselves independent actors on the revolutionary stage over the past ten months and Rawlings knew he would have to choose his moment carefully before moving against their leaders.

The opportunity came on 23 November when a number of disgruntled middle-ranking army officers, mainly from the north, staged a real coup attempt, with an attack on Gondar Barracks and mortars fired towards the Castle. Right-wing tendencies were believed to be involved in the attempt, and Brigadier Nunoo-Mensah chose this particularly critical moment to resign from the Council on the grounds that there was insufficient discipline within the organs of the revolusion. The coup attempt was quickly crushed and in his flush of victory Rawlings had the opportunity to rid his government of those left-wing conspirators who threatened not only to undermine the unity of the PNDC, but also to set up an alternative power-base among the PDCs and prevent any sensible economic recovery programme from being implemented. At a huge workers' durbar in Independence Square, which reaffirmed his leadership of the revolution, Rawlings linked the two conspiracies together and announced that the PNDC and the NDC would therefore need to be purged 'from top to bottom'. In a charge that was aimed directly at Atim, Akata-Pore and their colleagues in the JFM, Rawlings declared: 'the worst kind of enemy is the one who can speak the revolutionary language but can fool us.'

In the ensuing weeks, the left-wing ideologues of the JFM who had threatened to block the economic package were purged from the organs of government. The NDC was dissolved and restructured to bring the PDCs and WDCs under closer central control. Akata-Pore and several others were arrested while the remainder, Chris Atim among them, went into exile, convinced that Rawlings had betrayed all that the 31 December revolution had stood for.

Chapter 5

The Years of Recovery

While the left of the JFM and the People's Revolutionary League were plotting ways to overthrow Rawlings' leadership, Botchwey and the economic review committee were doing some empirical research to support their case for a radical re-evaluation of the cedi. They went to two of the principal exporting sectors, mining and timber, and asked various companies to calculate rigorously how much it cost each of them in cedis to produce a dollar's worth of exports. The results, just as the finance team suspected, revealed that it cost between fifteen and twenty cedis to produce one dollar's worth of gold or timber, and yet, for that dollar's worth, they were getting only ₵2.75 at the current rate of exchange. Cocoa was the same, as a result of which the Cocoa Marketing Board had run up a massive deficit of nearly ₵8 billion. The argument which was clearly supported by these figures, seems to have convinced all those in the Council and the Committee of Secretaries who had not already committed themselves to opposition through the October plot.

By December Botchwey was ready and in a nation-wide broadcast on 30 December 1982 he announced the basic principles and outline for a four-year Economic Recovery Programme (ERP). The devaluation issue was presented as a subsidy on specified exports – timber, minerals, cocoa, coffee and manufactured goods – while imports, apart from oil and basic foodstuffs were to be surcharged. The emphasis of the

ERP at this stage was upon increased production in agriculture and industry, combined with reducing the budget deficit by the cutting of government subsidies and more efficient collection of revenue.

In February the IMF accepted the programme as a sound basis for the advancement of credits and all that remained was to present the formal budget in April 1983, at which time people would find out how these proposals would affect their individual pockets. It was hoped that by then the government would have been able to gain support for the package in the country at large and convince people that, despite the departure of many prominent figures from the political left, the revolution was still on course.

As it turned out, the tough austerity budget planned for April 1983 could not have come at a worse time for the PNDC, for between the launch of the ERP in December and the budget in April, a number of other factors intervened, not the least important of which was a sudden and unexpected increase in the Ghanaian population by nearly 10 per cent.

On 17 January 1983 the Nigerian government announced that it was expelling within two weeks all foreign nationals without valid immigration documentation. Since Nigeria's oil-boom years of the 1970s, and Ghana's parallel decline, tens of thousands of Ghanaians had been migrating to Nigeria each year in search of work. It was dire economic necessity which drove them there. Most had intended it to be a temporary sojourn and so they avoided immigration controls, which at that time had been very slack. Now, in the dying months of the civilian regime, the Shagari government resorted to a popular emergency measure, supposedly designed to solve Nigeria's growing unemployment problems. At the same time it was interpreted in Ghana as part of a wider international programme for destabilising the Ghanaian revolution. The number of Ghanaians covered by the deportation order was estimated to be in excess of one million people and they were to be out of Nigeria by 2 February.

The PNDC responded immediately. It set up a special task force and despatched two ships of the Black Star Line to Lagos and a further one to Lomé in neighbouring Togo where it was known that many Ghanaians were heading in order to avoid harassment by Nigerian officials in Lagos. The first 'returnees', as they were known in Ghana, arrived aboard the *M.V.Sissili River* from Lomé in the early hours of Monday 24 January. By Wednesday 26th the *Sissili River* was back to pick up a further 300 000 from Lagos, where panic was setting in as the deadline drew near. The *Sissili River* had docked again in Tema by Thursday 27th and the other ships involved kept up a similar tight schedule.

On shore in Ghana the returnees were taken to a transit camp set up at the Trade Fair Site in Accra where for eighteen hours they were fed, processed and taken through medical checks. The government was determined that the problem of the returnees should not be allowed to develop into the sort of large-scale refugee problem which was a major drain on the limited resources of so many African countries. There was already some hostility towards the returnees from local Ghanaians who took the attitude that these people had deserted the country for richer pastures when times were hard and now their return to Ghana was likely to make a difficult economic situation even worse. The Rawlings' government, however, took the view that this was a humanitarian exercise which called for exceptional effort on behalf of the whole nation.

The PNDC called upon the self-help spirit of the revolution in its effort to involve every village in the country in helping their own sons and daughters in their time of need. Thus the returnees were dispersed to their home villages as soon as they had been processed at the Trade Fair. Those who had stayed true to their family responsibilities and sent home money during their time abroad were likely to fare better than those who had not done so. Rawlings himself headed a major propaganda effort to persuade everybody to co-operate. The private sector responded by donating funds and transport for the exercise and state corporations agreed to take on as many workers as they could. It was envisaged, however, that the vast majority would have to go to the rural areas, where most had come from in the first place, and be absorbed back into the farming sector. To this end Rawlings addressed the National House of Chiefs in Kumasi where he succeeded in persuading chiefs to make farming land available to all returnees who needed it.

The whole affair was a remarkable show of national communal spirit, exemplified at its best by the armada of thirty canoes which set out from Cape Coast, Elmina and neighbouring fishing villages on 1 February to bring back the last of the returnees. All told, in the space of just over two weeks, 1.2 million Ghanaians were evacuated home from Nigeria. Over the next few months, in an exercise which amazed the international aid agencies, Ghana managed to re-absorb into national life nearly one-tenth of her total population.

It was not without its cost, however. The economy was already in a state of major crisis, while in the drought-stricken countryside that was supposed to absorb all these people in productive work, bush fires were raging out of control, destroying thousands of hectares of productive crops, in particular many well-established cocoa farms.

It was under these circumstances that on Thursday 21 April 1983 the Secretary for Finance and Economic Planning, Dr Kwesi Botchwey, announced the toughest austerity budget of any government since independence. The minimum daily wage was nearly doubled from twelve cedis to just over twenty-one, and the prices of rice, maize and sugar remained unaltered, but virtually everything else went up by between 100 and 300 per cent as government subsidies were slashed to reduce the budget deficit and import surcharges were imposed on all but the most basic essentials. Thus meat rose from twenty cedis a kilo to eighty-three while the price of bottled beer doubled to twenty cedis and a packet of cigarettes likewise leaped to forty.

All over the country people were visibly shocked by the severity of the budget. There were several anti-government demonstrations and members of the economic management team, including Joe Abbey and Kwesi Botchwey, and the Secretary for Information were nearly lynched in Kumasi when they tried addressing a public meeting to explain the necessity for the budget. The strength of public outcry drove Rawlings to deliver an unusually long radio and television broadcast to the nation. He was careful not to gloss over the hardship that lay ahead, but sought to persuade the people that there was no alternative. The tone he took in this broadcast implicitly recognised that no ordinarily elected government of party politicians, with a necessary eye to the next election, would have been able to implement a package of measures so severe:

> If the PNDC government was concerned with cheap popularity, we would not have presented you with such a budget.
>
> It is hard to ask someone who has already tightened his belt to the last hole to go and make an additional hole to tighten it even further ... [but] the steady economic decline which has affected the country over the past decade has had to be arrested and the longer we wait, the harder it would be.

After several months of hectic public argument and with the continued support of the defence committees, the PNDC won reluctant acceptance of the budgetary measures from the majority of Ghanaians because they believed in the integrity of Rawlings and they saw the government's policy as directing wealth away from the rich and privileged and towards the rural farmers upon whom the wealth of the nation ultimately depended. What aided the working-class acceptance of the harshness of the ERP was the knowledge that even the middle-class and government functionaries were reduced to near penury.

The hardship of those years of 1982 and 1983 remain deeply ingrained in the Ghanaian collective memory. In almost every aspect of daily life, 1983 marked an historic low. In the cities the daily petrol queues from 3.00 a.m. dominated the life of many. Matches and toilet paper could not be bought for any money and people trekked on foot from store to store in search of a few kilos of rice or maize or a half-litre of palm oil. Groups of middle-class businessmen and professionals would sometimes group together and take a truck into the rural areas to try and buy yams, cassava or plantain. Even then they would have to travel from one village to another as the farmers themselves barely had enough to eat, let alone to sell. As inflation briefly soared to more than 100 per cent, civil servants, used to sending home money and other presents to support the family in the village, now suffered the indignity of having to beg parcels of food from aged parents in the rural areas.

While the middle-classes undoubtedly suffered hardship, the working class and the urban unemployed verged on starvation. *Kenkey*, the daily ration of maize-meal, traditionally sold cooked by street-side traders, was at times almost unobtainable. When it could be found, people were reduced to buying *kenkey* uncooked for fear that if they waited any longer there would be none left to buy. In mid-1983 the government imported 17 000 metric tons of cheap yellow maize, ostensibly for poultry feed, but in reality to sell for making *kenkey*. Government argued that it was just as good as white maize. The people, who knew better, had no option but to eat it. With malnutrition widespread and a shortage of drugs in hospitals and clinics, resistance to disease was lowered and for the first time in living memory people died in the streets of Accra.

During this particularly difficult time for everybody, the PNDC faced criticism from every direction. Students from the three universities, who had lost sympathy with the PNDC following the purge of the ultra left at the close of 1982, staged vociferous anti-government demonstrations in May 1983. The student position was ambivalent. Their revolutionary alliance with the working class had always been stronger in rhetoric than in daily life. In Kumasi there were violent clashes between students and organised groups of workers who saw their criticism of the PNDC as an attempt to subvert the people's revolution.

In response to this explosive situation, the PNDC took the draconian measure of closing all three universities for a year. Many members of the PNDC government had taken part as student leaders in the anti-UNIGOV demonstrations of 1977–78 which had helped bring down the Acheampong government. They were all too well aware of the danger of allowing the impetus of public protest to get beyond control. It was therefore prudent to nip the emergent opposition in the bud. Once more the occasion for the summary detention of many vocal critics of the government came in the wake of another abortive military coup.

There were several plots and attempted coups in 1983, the most serious one occurring on 19 June. In a dramatic repeat of November 1982, a number of people were sprung from Ussher Fort Prison, including most of those on trial for involvement in the November attempt. For about two hours a dozen rebel soldiers held Broadcasting House and regularly broadcast statements claiming that Rawlings and the PNDC had been overthrown. Once again, however, the bulk of the ranks remained loyal to the PNDC and a member of Rawlings' personal security guard from Gondar Barracks brought up a fearsome new 106 mm recoil-less cannon which most people even in the armed forces were not aware the country possessed. This was used to fire eight high explosive rockets in quick succession through the gates of Broadcasting House with a noise that was heard throughout the city. As the rebels fled, a breathless Captain Quashigah made his way to the broadcasting studio and announced that the situation was under control. Quashigah became the hero of the hour although he was later to fall out with Rawlings, develop his own ambitions and be arrested for plotting a coup in 1989.

An ominous and unpredictable element in the opposition to Rawlings and the PNDC during the early years of the revolution was the clandestine involvement of the United States' Central Intelligence Agency (CIA). Early in 1983 documents came into the hands of Special Security Adviser Captain Kojo Tsikata which showed clear CIA involvement with dissident Ghanaians who were trying to destabilise and overthrow the PNDC regime. It came at the height of US attempts to subvert the Nicaraguan government, with whose revolution the PNDC felt a strong sense of solidarity. Ghana's close links with Libya and the PNDC Chairman's fearless anti-imperialist rhetoric all helped to make Rawlings one of a select group of *bêtes noires* of Reaganite foreign policy. In most of the abortive coup attempts against the PNDC during 1983 and 1984 the hand of the CIA was to be found lurking somewhere, providing weapons, money or contacts through their offices at the US embassy in Accra or in Lomé.

In July 1985 a female African-American officer of the CIA, recently returned from Accra, was arrested in Washington on suspicion of passing secret documents to the government of Ghana. Arrested with her was her supposed Ghanaian contact, Mike Soussoudis, who happened to be a cousin of Chairman Rawlings. The documents which had come into the hands of the PNDC gave the names of American CIA agents and Ghanaians working for the CIA as well as the activities of Ghanaian dissidents in Lomé and elsewhere. On the basis of this information the government was able to arrest a number of Ghanaians in Accra who had been working at the US embassy. Four of these were put on trial in November 1985. They admitted passing information to the Americans and were sentenced to terms of imprisonment. There then followed the extraordinary sight of the Ghanaian government arranging a spy-swap with the US government in which eight CIA agents were stripped of their Ghanaian citizenship and exchanged for Mike Soussoudis, still being held in Washington. Soussoudis arrived home to a hero's welcome in December 1985.

Regardless of the Ghanaian government's solidly-structured and Western-backed economic recovery programme, in place since 1983, US intelligence service personnel continued their subversive activities against the PNDC. It was not until the late 1980s and after the US raid on Tripoli in 1986 that US foreign policy advisers began to lessen their suspicions that Rawlings' PNDC was part of a Libyan-sponsored anti-Western conspiracy.

Despite the niggling persistence of external hostility, from the historic low of 1983, conditions in Ghana could only improve. Much of the credit for the country's recovery in the years that followed must be laid at the doors of the Ghanaian people themselves, whose courage, faith and determination was what made any economic revival possible. The government deserves the credit for taking the necessary difficult decisions in economic policy and implementing them with clarity of vision, although critics would say that this was relatively straightforward for a government that had come to power through the barrel of a gun and had no electorate to answer to. Even the PNDC, however, could not have carried through such a fundamental restructuring programme without the acceptance and co-operation of the mass of the Ghanaian people. Co-operation of this level could never have been gained by fear alone. It was won in no small measure by the people's belief in the integrity of the Chairman of the PNDC, Flight Lieutenant Jerry Rawlings.

Although the old establishment of middle-class businessmen and professionals feared and distrusted Rawlings and the PNDC, as they would almost any military or 'revolutionary' government, the mass of ordinary Ghanaians believed that he was there for them. The 'ruling class' were no longer indulging in conspicuous consumption whilst the mass of Ghanaians starved, and people widely believed they had Jerry Rawlings to thank for that.

Signs of economic recovery began to show in 1984, helped by a year of reasonable rains which saw good harvests throughout the rural areas. The major emphasis of PNDC policy from the beginning was upon the strongest sector of the economy, peasant agriculture. Apart from regularly raising produce prices – cocoa prices to the farmer were raised 700 per cent in the first five years of the revolution – the PNDC had already in 1982 taken the important step of introducing a system of direct payment to cocoa farmers. Previously farmers had received a promissory chit from the CMB which the farmers were sometimes not able to get exchanged into cash for several months. Now farmers were paid by cheque at the point of weighing-in their produce. This *'akuafo'* cheque could be lodged in a bank account and immediately drawn upon. Initially this presented problems as most farmers did not have bank accounts and there were only 120 bank branches in the whole country. Over subsequent years, however, this situation has steadily improved. Farmers have become used to using banks, the number of bank branches has increased, including rural banks, and the *akuafo* cheque system has been extended to other agricultural products.

By 1985 the effects of the government's firm assertion of control over the economy were plain for all to see. Inflation, that important indicator of economic health, fell from 120 per cent in 1983 to 37 per cent in 1984 and 10.4 per cent in 1985. Thereafter, as economic activity revived across all sectors, inflation failed to fall any further and from 1986 to 1991 it floated between 20 and 37 per cent. Meanwhile, that other basic economic indicator, Gross Domestic Product, has maintained an impressive annual growth of about 5 per cent: double that of most sub-Saharan African countries.

Whereas in mid-1982 three-quarters of all Ghana's foreign exchange was spent on crude oil imports and most of the rest on food, by 1989 only one-fifth of foreign exchange was going on oil. The rest went to finance imports for the re-development of the industrial, transport, agricultural and construction sectors. Barely one-tenth was going on food imports.

Things seemed to be going quite well by 1985 and many in the government would have been happy to coast along for a while enjoying the fruits of modest recovery. The Chairman, however, was not prepared to let things slide. At a moment when most people needed a rest from hard times and personal sacrifice, Rawlings listened to the arguments of his economic advisers and agreed to the launching of ERP Mark II. He used all his personal standing to push it through the Council and the Committee of Secretaries.

The recovery programme now moved towards a major restructuring exercise. A start was made on a fundamental overhaul of the banking and revenue system. In addition, the over-weighty civil service needed serious trimming and over the next few years some 40 000 people were redeployed from the civil service. Many went into farming, but others were retrained for work in the manufacturing and maintenance industries. Similarly, 20 000 were redeployed from state corporations and government began a divestment programme from direct state involvement in agriculture and industry.

Steps to 'liberalise' the economy were paralleled by moves to bring the exchange rate mechanism further into line with market rates. Instead of the previous practice of periodic large devaluations over several years, in September 1986 the Ghanaian government went over to a system of weekly auctions where bankers and traders could bid for foreign exchange at regular market rates. This introduced a gradual slide in exchange rate variation until by 1990 some kind of stability had become established. Foreign exchange (forex) bureaux were opened in cities and major towns where anybody could go and buy or sell the foreign exchange they needed at the going market rate. This abolished virtually at a stroke the illegal parallel market in foreign exchange which had so badly undermined economic stability in earlier years.

Government borrowing from World Bank and other major donor agencies has, of course, been fundamental to any economic recovery, and critics of the PNDC fear that the government is accumulating a massive debt to hang around the neck of future generations. Unlike former political regimes, however, the PNDC has been careful to keep a check on irresponsible government spending. Thus loans are not being accumulated simply to prop up an unwieldy civil service and inefficient state corporations. Although there is much reform still needed in both these sectors, the bulk of government borrowing has been directed towards rebuilding the infrastructure of the country, thus providing the basic facilities without which long-term economic development is impossible.

Rehabilitation of the country's infrastructure has been led by the $73 million modernisation of Tema and Takoradi ports, a project begun in 1987 with assistance from the World Bank. This was followed by investment in road repair, rehabilitation and upgrading. Irrigation projects were initiated in Upper East Region as early as 1985 and since then efforts have been made to extend potable water facilities and electricity to every district capital. This ambitious project of investment has a long way to go, with 40 per cent of district capitals still without electricity, but at least a start has been made, a comprehensive plan is in position and the national grid now stretches narrowly into the Northern and Upper East Regions.

A vital part of a country's infrastructure is its educational system, for education has the power to shape a nation's cultural character as well as ensure its long-term social and economic well-being. Recognising the importance of education in strengthening the emerging self-reliant consciousness of the Ghanaian people, the PNDC has characteristically grasped this thorny problem firmly in its hands and set about a fundamental reform of Ghana's educational system. While the admirably high standards of the country's tertiary institutions had, over the years, won Ghana's graduates international recognition and enabled her doctors and engineers to compete successfully on the international stage, the pyramidal structure of the system had ensured that the vast majority were excluded from these heights of privilege and most became educational 'drop-outs' at an early stage. The challenge facing the PNDC was to re-orientate the system away from its academic focus to benefit the majority and to render Ghanaian education more socially and economically relevant to the realities of everyday life in modern Ghana.

Experimental schools had been tried in the mid-1970s and plans for reform had long been in the air, but any serious progress on educational restructuring had met with resistance from the influential tertiary sector as well as from educational professionals and civil servants. Even when the PNDC began to tackle the problem in the late 1980s they were accused of rushing things and being ill-prepared. Nevertheless, they pushed ahead. Focusing on content as well as structure and with the emphasis on basic skills, they widened the educational net, inaugurated Junior Secondary Schools in 1987 and introduced a whole new range of practical and cultural subjects to the curriculum, including more science and technology, life skills, cultural studies and compulsory Ghanaian languages. At the same time the entry qualifications for the tertiary sector were adapted to take account of the changes, and this is where most of the resistance still resides. Although some may attempt to make educational reform a political football during 1992, most are coming to terms with the changes and beginning to appreciate the positive contribution which the reformed educational institutions can make to the long-term development of the nation.

An important aspect of Ghana's economic recovery, not so obvious to the casual observer, has been the awakening of a sense of personal responsibility for the future welfare of the country. No longer do people simply assume the attitude fostered by the early Nkrumah years: that government will provide. One of the clearest manifestations of this new individual attitude has been in the field of personal taxation. In 1983 the government's revenue department was collecting little more than 4 per cent of Gross National Product in taxation. By 1989 this figure had risen to 16 per cent. The turnaround began in 1982 with the activities of the Citizen's Vetting Committee (CVC).

The CVC had been established at the beginning of the revolution, early in 1982. At that time the brunt of personal taxation was borne by the salaried wage earners whose tax was deducted at source by their employers. A large percentage of potential government revenue was simply lost through tax evasion by the bulk of the self-employed who paid virtually no income tax at all. The lower ranks of the military who had staged the revolution saw the issue in simplistic terms: the rich were the cause of their poverty; therefore the rich must be caught and brought to justice. The establishment of the CVC appeared to take account of their political aspirations, for a 'citizen' in those early months was by definition 'an enemy of the revolution'.

The initial terms of reference of the CVC were to investigate the lifestyles of certain categories of people, such as anybody with more than one car or with a bank balance

17 Demonstration in support of the 31 December revolution

Anna Tully/PANOS Pictures

18 Students help evacuate the cocoa harvest, January 1982

Ministry of Information

19 Chris Atim, member of the PNDC, launching a Workers' Defence Committee, February 1982
Ministry of Information

20 Chairman of the PNDC, J.J. Rawlings, at the OAU Summit, Tripoli, August 1982, with Sam Nujoma and Colonel Gaddafi
Ministry of Information

21 Ghanaian deportees boarding the *Sissili River* at Lagos, January 1983

People's Daily Graphic

22 Chairman Rawlings, Joyce Aryee, Secretary for Information and Captain Quashigah after the successful crushing of the abortive coup attempt of 19 June 1983

People's Daily Graphic

23 Chairman Rawlings talking to some children on a visit to a rural school

Anna Tully/PANOS Pictures

24 Passing out parade at Ghana Military Academy. Behind the Head of State stands Major-General W.M. Mensah-Wood, General Officer Commanding the Ghana Armed Forces and member of the PNDC

Ministry of Information

25 J.J. Rawlings and Thomas Sankara taking a salute on the northern border region between Ghana and Burkina Faso

People's Daily Graphic

26 Captain Kojo Tsikata (rtd.), PNDC member with special responsibility for security and foreign affairs, in discussion with Yasser Arafat, Chairman of the Palestine Liberation Organisation, 1986

Ministry of Information

27 Chairman Rawlings meeting farmers at a Farmer's Day, Wenchi, Brong-Ahafo Region, March 1991

Ministry of Information

28 Nana Konadu Agyeman Rawlings, wife of the Head of State and leader of the 31 December Women's Movement

Ministry of Information

29 A District Assembly in progress, Tepa, April 1991
Ministry of Local Government

30 Speakers from the floor addressing one of the regional fora on 'Evolving a True Democracy', 1990
Ministry of Information

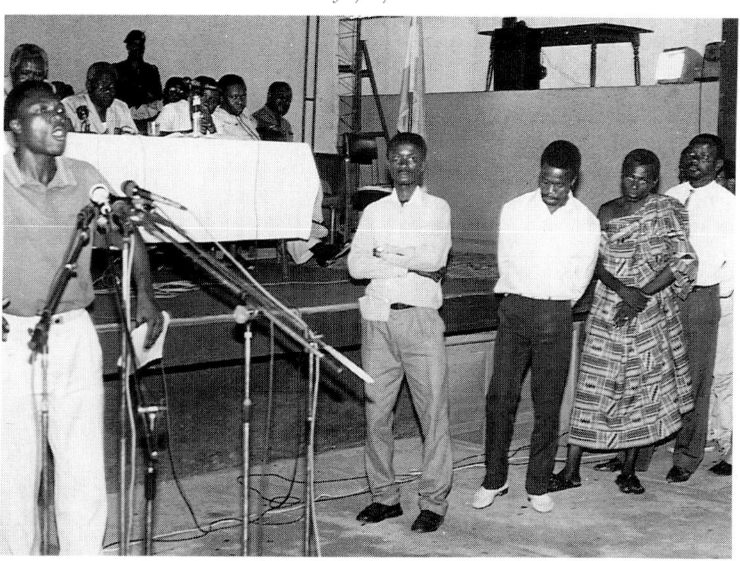

31 Chairman Rawlings on his first official visit to a western European country, with President Mitterand of France, Paris, July 1991
Ministry of Information

32 Chairman Rawlings at the conference of the Non-Aligned Movement, Accra, September 1991
Ministry of Information

of more than ₵50 000. A census was taken of the ownership of houses, offices and warehouses and a record was kept of anybody who travelled by air. The committee's investigations concentrated on those involved in trade, distribution and services. These were the areas which in previous years had been so profitable. Very little investigation was made of those clearly engaged in industrial and agricultural production as these were the sectors of the economy which the government was keen to promote. Inevitably, the brunt of the early investigations fell heavily upon the lawyers and businessmen who had formed part of the prosperous establishment of the Third Republic, and this laid the CVC open to the accusation that it was conducting a vindictive witch-hunt along the lines of the AFRC. The activities of the CVC, however, were very different from the crude attempts to curb corruption which had characterised the AFRC period. The committee itself was properly constituted and was very professional in the conduct of its affairs. It had on its board, representatives of the Church, the legal profession, the military, an accountant, a tax expert and a quantity-surveyor.

Initially the CVC focused on obvious tax evasion by the wealthy, and huge arrears of revenue were collected in its first two years of operation. By 1984/85 it had enough information for a major restructuring of the financial system, at which point it had served its initial purpose as a vetting committee. The government now set up a task force to look at the whole system of revenue collection and out of the former government revenue department it created a new autonomous Internal Revenue Service.

The system that was now introduced for tax collection had been stumbled upon by the CVC when it was investigating a trader in Volta Region who owned several warehouse buildings. So far as this woman was concerned only nurses, teachers and civil servants paid income tax. Traders paid rates on their property and that was all. It was an attitude which was widespread in society as a whole and had been allowed to persist more or less since independence. Everybody expected the government to provide a whole range of social and economic facilities, but little or no thought was given as to where the money came from. The CVC had in effect unearthed a level of tax consciousness which was so low as to be virtually non-existent. However, once this particular trader had been persuaded of her financial obligations, she proposed:'We traders know each other and each other's business. If you want the taxes to be collected properly and fairly, let us do it for you.' It was the germ of an idea for self-help taxation which was to transform the tax collection system from the self-employed.

Each group of self-employed – petty-traders, taxi-drivers, fetish priests – formed their own 'association'. The Internal Revenue Service then appointed agents from these associations to collect taxes from their own members. They knew their members and they were the people best placed to bring them into the tax-paying system. In due course, in 1987, lorry and taxi drivers' associations requested to be allowed to pay their taxes on a daily basis rather than in an annual lump sum. Thus developed the system whereby each driver must carry on him when he is working, a daily tax receipt, showing that he is paid-up for the day, and produce it when requested by members of the drivers' association who mount occasional road-side checks.

After some initial teething problems, the system, as it developed, worked well, so well in fact that the World Bank, which had provided some early funding, described it as a 'revenue miracle' and proposed to try to introduce it into Uganda.

On the financial front the PNDC made public display of the extent of Ghana's economic recovery in June 1990 when the government paid off in full the $600 million of foreign exchange arrears which had accumulated before the ERP was launched. It was a dramatic statement of confidence in the future which evoked a reciprocal response from the international donor agencies when they met in Paris in May 1991. They pledged more in soft loans and grants for Ghana than the Ghanaian delegation had even asked for.

Although in macro-economic terms the government's recovery programme undoubtedly looks impressive, the PNDC is still a long way from creating the strong and self-reliant economy which Dr Kwesi Botchwey set out as the revolution's objective in 1982. To a large extent Ghana's is still a neo-colonial economy, dependent for its continued growth upon the vagaries of the international commodity market. In 1977, for instance, the world market price for cocoa had stood at a record £3000 a ton. By 1987 this had fallen to £1500 and two years later it was down to little more than £600. On the other hand, during the same period the price of most imports and the general cost of living in Ghana has continued to rise. Planning for sustained growth under these circumstances is extremely difficult and the Ghanaian economy remains in a very fragile state.

Nevertheless, in terms of what the PNDC set out to do in 1982, namely, to place production at the forefront of economic policy and to raise production in every sector, the recovery programme has achieved remarkable results. The three traditional export commodities – cocoa, timber and gold – have all shown marked increases in production. Cocoa, which totalled 258 000 metric tonnes in the 1981/82 season and fell to 160 000 tonnes in 1983/84, rose to a steady 300 000 tonnes a year from 1989 to 1991. The timber industry suffered considerable management problems during the 1980s, with the persistence of corrupt practices in invoicing. This has particularly frustrated Chairman Rawlings who seemed initially to assume that one could simply wipe out misdeeds by decree. However, most of the timber operations have now been brought under firm control and the industry has grown from strength to strength. From $20 million worth of exports in 1981 and less than $15 million worth in 1982, the timber industry achieved returns worth $134 million in 1990.

The one sector of the economy that has managed to attract substantial foreign capital investment is mining. Stimulated by this investment, gold, diamonds, bauxite and manganese have all expanded considerably since 1985. Gold, in particular, is thriving in the early 1990s, with Ashanti Goldfields alone producing over half a million ounces annually and the Southern Cross company expecting to add a further 100 000 ounces in 1991.

More significant in the long term for the health of the Ghanaian economy has been the growth and diversification of what are known as non-traditional exports. These have expanded not only vertically, from a value of $10 million in 1981 to $60 million in 1990, but also horizontally. From the former staples of timber products, pineapples, salt and kola nuts, the range has now broadened to include shea-nuts, cocoa butter and a wide variety of horticultural products for the 'ethnic market' in Europe – mangoes, limes, yams and other roots, smoked fish, water melon and medicinal plants.

There remains, however, a substantial weakness in Ghana's developing economy. The country has still not developed a strong enough processing industry, both to meet her own consumer needs and to export as high-value finished products. It is only in this direction that long-term economic stability can be achieved and sustained. The government hopes to attract more foreign private capital to expand the manufacturing sector of the economy, but ultimately where investment must come from is indigenous Ghanaian capital.

With the PNDC still not having altogether thrown off the 'anti-wealth' rhetoric of the revolution, many potential Ghanaian investors, both at home and abroad, are still hesitant to risk their all in private manufacturing. The prospect of constitutional government in a Fourth Republic should help in this direction.

In the meantime, on the human and individual economic front, things have been very hard for the vast majority of Ghanaians, as the government itself is prepared to concede. Rawlings summed up his recognition of this fact in a New Year broadcast to the nation on 2 January 1990:

> I should be the first to admit that the Economic Recovery Programme has not provided all the answers to our national problems. In spite of all the international acclaim it has received, the effects of its gains remain to be felt in most households and pockets.

After eight years of recovery and macro-economic growth, the vast majority of Ghanaians are still very poor. The cost of living is prohibitively high in relation to the basic wage. The unskilled casual labourer earns barely enough to feed himself while teachers, nurses and civil servants find it hard to make ends meet and many engage in extra part-time work. With the notable exception of a small minority in the business community and in private professional practice, people basically have had to learn to live on less. A heavy burden for families is the cost of health and education. The cost of schooling has increased. Although tuition is still free, there are fees for every other aspect of school life. The fees for food, drugs and clinic attendance in hospitals are high; but at least the hospitals now have drugs. As many have come to realise, what use is a totally free health service if it provides no service ? At least the factories can now get raw materials, shops have foodstuffs and the transport services can get spare parts, even if it is at a heavy cost.

Ghanaians are no longer cushioned from the harsh world of international economics; but at the same time they are not being blatantly exploited by their rulers or subjected to the corruption and mismanagement of former years. The civil service is still cumbersome, slow and reluctant to relinquish the kind of power to the districts that had been envisaged in the early days of the revolution; but the ministries are now being systematically restructured and much has been achieved in streamlining their activities. Some corruption still exists, but it is no longer all pervasive, no longer an automatic fact of life. With the strong anti-corruption lead of Chairman Rawlings and the number of prosecutions by Public Tribunals, people now think twice before they engage in a corrupt deal or wield their influence to favour a relative. What is more, people are more prepared to stand up and challenge any corruption when they are subjected to it. Foreign investors and contractors in particular have learned the hard way that they can no longer divert valuable foreign loans into their own private pockets just through offering a percentage to some senior government official.

In the rural areas the farmers generally have been receiving higher prices for their crops, although life is still extremely hard. In recognition of the heavy impact which the economic recovery and structural adjustment programmes have had on the poorest sectors of the community, the government, with help from outside aid, has embarked upon a remarkable 'Programme of Action to Mitigate the Social Cost of Adjustment' (PAMSCAD).

PAMSCAD, begun in January 1989, was originally limited to one thousand projects, identified as a result of local community initiative. People in the villages were asked to identify their local needs, which might include repair and rehabilitation of Primary School buildings, building of new health posts and pit-latrines, digging wells, desilting dams, or constructing short access roads. As far as possible these projects were to be based on local labour, local technology and local materials. Once the project had been identified and detailed proposals drawn up, government would seek the finance from specific international aid agencies which had already pledged funds for PAMSCAD projects. In due course PAMSCAD became involved in meeting other social needs, especially in the remoter rural areas. These included supplementary feeding programmes for lactating mothers, de-worming of more than one million children between the ages of six and twelve, enhancing opportunities for women in development, helping re-deployees to settle into agriculture and providing food for public works programmes in Northern and Upper Regions.

Although often slated by critics of the government as too little done too late, through PAMSCAD the PNDC has not only added a new acronym to the vocabulary of international aid, but it has initiated a new consciousness of the need for local self-help in the rural areas of Ghana which can only augur well for the future of the country.

The Ghanaian workers who seem to have fared least well under the PNDC have been the low-paid wage-earners of the urban areas. The minimum wage level was badly affected by the ultra-high inflation of the early 1980s and, despite regular hikes since then, it has failed to raise the standard of living for the majority of urban workers. Many wonder where is their share of the much-heralded 5 per cent growth rate!

The TUC has come to an arrangement with the PNDC that many people feel is 'too cosy' for the comfort of the workers. Minimum wage levels are now negotiated at tripartite meetings between government, employers and the TUC. In return, the individual unions are expected to curb their confrontational inclinations. Certainly, in contrast to the record of previous governments, the decade of PNDC rule has been, on the surface, one of relative peace in industrial relations. This, however, has probably been more to do with the firm stance of government, than with the level of worker satisfaction. Despite its original revolutionary rhetoric, the PNDC has not been a government to tolerate industrial unrest.

Workers at the Ghana Broadcasting Corporation (GBC), for instance, learned this to their cost in 1988 when they staged a demonstration in support of five of their dismissed colleagues. The demonstrators managed to stop radio transmission for four hours on 1 November 1988, but then armed police were sent in, numerous workers were arrested and fifteen GBC union leaders were dismissed. The PNDC has taken similar summary action against petroleum workers who tried to halt production at the Tema oil refinery. Here again, the confrontation was followed by widespread dismissals. Clearly, the PNDC has its own definition of what constitutes the workers' interests when a strategic sector of the economy is threatened with disruption. Because the lid has been kept so firmly upon industrial unrest over the past decade, however, a future democratically-elected government, lacking the draconian powers of the PNDC, is going to have to come to terms with the overdue expectations of a disillusioned urban work force.

6

The Rawlings Factor

On Friday 16 December 1983 Flight Lieutenant J.J.Rawlings led a high-level Ghanaian delegation on a one-day working visit to neighbouring Côte d'Ivoire. They landed at the up-country airport of Yamoussoukro, birth-place of the 78-year-old Ivorian President, Houphouët-Boigny. They were met with a resounding welcome. As Rawlings stepped from his aircraft he was mobbed by wildly enthusiastic crowds, among them many Ghanaian nationals and several hundred Togolese who had travelled up from Abidjan to cheer their hero, J.J.Rawlings. The crowds set up an incessant clapping chant which followed the Ghanaian Head of State all the way to the Ivorian President's palace:

> J.J.! [*clap, clap*]
> J.J.! [*clap, clap*]
> Do something
> Before you die!

It was a chant which was to be picked up and become popular back in Ghana, especially among school children in the rural areas. It is used in many mass spontaneous greetings of the Chairman of the PNDC when he lands by helicopter in remote rural villages, especially in the Northern, Western or Brong-Ahafo Regions.

The popularity of Rawlings in neighbouring African countries is something that has never ceased to amaze

Ghanaians and worry other African heads of government. The admiration stems partly from Rawlings' heroic stand against corrupt authority back in May 1979, a stand which was reinforced by the AFRC's subsequent execution of several former rulers for corruption. The PNDC's ousting of the old ruling élite in December 1981 merely confirmed the idea in many people's minds that here was a man who understood the aspirations of the common man. In the years since the launching of the 31 December revolution, Rawlings' clear concern for the poor and the exploited and his declarations of revolutionary 'power to the people' have been an intoxicating brew, much sought after in the autocratically-ruled countries of neighbouring West Africa.

Rawlings is a larger-than-life character who has fascinated admirers and opponents ever since his first appearance on the political scene in 1979. He has been the principal subject of several books, including one published in Germany under a title which translates into English as *A Piece of Madness*. The author, Elke Molke, appears unable to make up her mind whether she is writing a work of fact or a piece of romantic fiction.

The book is set in the turbulent days of 1979 when the author was in fact the wife of a German diplomat stationed in Accra. She did indeed know Rawlings, having met him at the Recce riding stables in the early part of 1979, and the 'piece of madness' of the title is the author's reputed relationship with the Rawlings' character, 'Jerry Johnson'. But throughout the book the boundaries between fact and fiction remain deliberately blurred. Many of the publicly-known facts of the June 4th Revolution are related in the style of a diary and most of the central characters of the drama are given their correct names. In an interesting aside, however, Boakye Djan becomes 'Quakye Djan', the blood-thirsty 'Communist' who pulls the strings behind the scenes, the required evil genius of romantic fiction. Where the book most clearly reveals the prejudicial viewpoint of the author is in its portrayal of Rawlings as an amoral, drug-crazed womaniser, a practiser of 'voodoo' who is so unsure of himself, so ignorant of African culture and the basic concepts of justice and democracy, that he needs to be taught them by the author from her patronising heights of intellect. In his own country, however, the aspirations and the actions of Jerry Rawlings have, over the years, been subjected to far more thorough scrutiny, from which emerges a character both more complex and more credible. Rawlings is a man of strong emotions who is driven by a passion for moral justice and any honest assessment of the man must acknowledge his intellect and integrity.

On the intellectual front there are those who maintain that Rawlings has been the first Ghanaian leader of charisma and of stature since Nkrumah in his earliest years. They argue, and with good reason, that the undoubted achievements of the past ten years have only been possible because of the Rawlings factor; that it is Rawlings more than any other individual who has led them through the difficult years of economic recovery and given Ghanaians back their national pride and self-respect. For every fervent admirer, however, there is a fierce critic and opponent.

Opposition to Rawlings stems from many quarters. The obvious opponents are those whom Rawlings overthrew in 1981. For them, the 31 December revolution challenged all they believed in and stood for in the established constitutional system. The concept of 'people's power' was anathema to them and the bitter pill became all the harder to swallow when Rawlings was seen to be implementing the sort of Western-backed recovery programme which they felt they could have implemented themselves if only they had been allowed the chance. It is high irony indeed that they of all people should accuse Rawlings of betraying the revolutionary rhetoric of his original 'Holy War'.

From a very different perspective, former revolutionary colleagues, many of them now in exile, similarly accuse

Rawlings of betraying the ideals of the revolution. The principal grounds for this accusation, stemming as it does from the left wing of the early movement, is the PNDC's turning to the IMF and the World Bank for the necessary funds to finance the country's economic recovery. They see in this the signs of capitalist conspiracy and conclude that Rawlings, for all his revolutionary rhetoric of 1981 and early 1982, is in fact no more than a personally ambitious tool of capitalist imperialism. To maintain such an attitude over many years, however, is to ignore the realities of the man as well as the harsh realities of economic life.

In 1979, judging by his public utterances, Rawlings viewed his politics in very simple terms. He saw the symbols of the oppression that he hated, but he saw them in the personalities of the exploiters: corruption was the action of greedy and amoral individuals, not part of a system which had removed the old constraints on what was right and what was wrong. The execution of the senior officers and the blowing up of Makola market were to Rawlings regrettable necessities: necessary on the one hand to calm the angry rank and file, and on the other hand to stand as symbols for the ending of the old order of corruption and exploitation. The most important achievement of the June 4th period in Rawlings' view was the restoration of the dignity of the people. The ranks had challenged their 'superior' officers; and their example had been taken up in spirit if not in fact by the civilians in the streets and in the factories.

When Rawlings handed over power on 24 September 1979, it was, officially, on the understanding that the incoming politicians would live up to their promises to continue the 'house cleaning process'. While he appears to have trusted the integrity of Dr Hilla Limann whom he saw as an honest man, right from the start of the Third Republic he must have had his doubts about the party politicians and their financial backers who once more saw themselves in the ascendancy. Their subsequent actions and inaction, their inability or unwillingness to solve the country's problems and finally the evident corruption in public office, justified in Rawlings' mind the suspension of the whole electoral system.

During the days of the Third Republic the security service's harassment of Rawlings and his companions and the judiciary's attacks upon the judgements of the AFRC merely helped Rawlings to identify himself more closely with the poor and the oppressed. Those who persuaded him to join and head the June Fourth Movement, however, were just as guilty of using the Rawlings name, his populist appeal and his ability to effect a coup, as he was guilty of using the platform of a left-wing organisation when he himself was not a committed Marxist.

Rawlings was undoubtedly impressed by the intellectual arguments of the political left in the JFM and elsewhere, but it is clear that he remained throughout an essentially practical man. He knew that if the rulers of the Third Republic made 'violent revolution inevitable' and he returned to power, then he must restructure society to exclude the present ruling élite from their domination of the affairs of men. The radical intellectuals proposed a system of grass-roots participation in the decision-making process through the establishment of people's defence committees and it was this basic sense of people's accountability which must have appealed to Rawlings. He believed in people standing up for themselves, directing their own affairs and no longer being exploited and deprived of dignity by corrupt and self-serving politicians, landlords or employers. His was a moral revolution as much as a social and economic one. It was not for nothing that he termed the 31 December revolution a 'Holy War'.

The Rawlings who returned to power on 31 December 1981 was a far more cool-headed, logic-driven leader than the highly emotional young officer of 1979 who rode the tiger of the June 4th Revolution on his instinct and adrenalin.

Although he accepted most of the practical proposals of the intellectual left, Rawlings was not a man to be tied to ideological argument. To this extent he was never a 'Marxist' in the intellectual sense. Rawlings was not a great reader of books and those he did read, such as Franz Fanon's *Wretched of the Earth* and Paulo Freire's *Pedagogy of the Oppressed*, served more to confirm his own ideas on life and social justice than to influence him in any specific ideological direction. Certain socialistic systems, as evolved for instance in Cuba, Nicaragua or Libya, gave power to the people and were therefore useful reference points; but when it came to practical economics, he was just as open to other ideas. Thus he followed and accepted the arguments of his economic advisers. He saw the necessity for budgetary balance, and unlike many of his intellectual colleagues, he saw the need to come to terms with the harsh realities of exchange rate imbalance and its long-term drain upon the country's wealth. This is what led him to pursue with such dogged determination the immensely unpopular terms of the economic recovery programme, launched as it was at the height of the economic crisis of 1983. Having made the decision, he had the courage and the strength of character to stick with it, although the other side of that determination was his intolerance of those who now opposed him. He perceived theirs as the vacuous arguments of those who sought to evade reality and impose an impractical economic experiment for the sake of ideology.

Because of his firm stand on the economic issues, Rawlings was destined thereafter to face the accusation that he had betrayed the original goals of the revolution, to which he replied in an interview with the *People's Daily Graphic* in March 1987:

> Our revolutionary goals are constant. They have not changed and will not change ...

> We are not parlour theoreticians. All our actions have been based on realism and the hard facts of our economic situation. Given the resources at our disposal, and the current international economic atmosphere, we could not have come all this way without the financial support of the World Bank, the International Monetary Fund, and other countries. But we have not swallowed hook, line and sinker all the prescriptions of the multi-national financial institutions . . .
>
> We are on a long journey. We could refuse any help, and thereby compel our people to crawl slowly and more painfully along the road to recovery. If we want to speed up the process and ride part of the way in a bus, then we must pay the fare.

The strength of character and determination with which Rawlings has pushed through and stuck to the economic recovery programme has shown its face in other aspects of his rule. By all accounts he can be a difficult man to work with because he demands of his colleagues in government the same energy and commitment that he himself is willing to give. He very rarely offers praise to Council members or Secretaries of State for his attitude is that they are simply there to do their job. At the same time he has a fiery temper and he has been known to explode with rage at what he considers to be incompetence or laziness. It must be said that he leads so strongly from the front, and his is such a dominant and passionate personality, that many are afraid to disagree with him.

Those who have consistently disagreed with Rawlings have learned the consequences to their cost. Boakye Djan, who worked closely with him on the Council of the AFRC, has pointed out that none of the members of the Council of June 1979 remained with Rawlings to reappear on the PNDC in January 1982; and that none of the original members of the PNDC remained on Council very long.

Although this is strictly true, it is equally true that a considerable number of people who were behind the scenes and on the fringes of the AFRC in 1979, re-emerged in similar roles in 1982 and many of those have remained in government for most of the Rawlings' decade.

Boakye Djan's point, however, is that Rawlings is unreliable, inconsistent and an impossible man to work with: someone who must always have his own way. Others, who have worked with Rawlings through the years of PNDC rule maintain that he is open to persuasion, provided the arguments are clearly formulated and adhered to. Most agree that once Rawlings is convinced that he is right, it is very difficult to shift him and, because of his fiery temper, few are prepared to try. What to him may appear to be firm decision-making, others will see as evidence of Rawlings running a 'one-man-show'!

The Chairman normally allows himself to be guided by the collective decisions of Council and the Committee of Secretaries. He does not actually chair Council Meetings and only intervenes in matters regarding the mechanics of achieving objectives or other tactical considerations. There have been occasions, however, when he appears to be dictatorial in his use of executive power. PNDC Law 24, which defines the executive powers of government, stipulates that any decision taken by the Chairman and one other member of the Council constitutes a decision of the PNDC. In practice this gives Rawlings virtual sole executive authority as it is rare for a single member of Council to challenge his decision once he has made up his mind on an issue.

A well-known occasion when he exerted this authority, without consulting the Council, was the sacking of Aanaa Enin in October 1989. Mrs Aanaa Enin was at the time the longest-serving member of the Council, apart from the Chairman himself, and the manner of her dismissal suggests that personal rather than policy issues were at stake. The official reason given for her dismissal was 'conduct incompatible with revolutionary humility'! It appears that her relationships with those she worked with had been deteriorating for some time, to the great concern of government. Nevertheless, considering her length of service, other members of the government were unhappy with the manner of her dismissal. Had members of government been consulted, it is doubtful whether they would have wished to be a part of the decision to discipline her in such harsh terms.

It is in Rawlings' character, however, to speak his mind whenever he feels something very strongly. Thus he has been known, when making a formal public speech, to push aside his prepared text and launch into a tirade against someone whom he considers has been unjust or who for one reason or another deserves his criticism. On such occasions his colleagues in the government cringe at the thought of what he may come out with next while his audience lean forward in eager anticipation of some startling revelation. A famous example was his attack upon the Catholic hierarchy in June 1985 on the occasion of the commissioning of the Ghana Broadcasting Corporation's new transmitters.

Rawlings had for several years grown increasingly concerned about the Catholic Church's attitude towards the PNDC and the revolution. He had always admired the work of those priests and missionaries whom he knew to be devoting themselves wholeheartedly to living and working with the poor. It was this sort of work which he had envisaged for himself when in his early adult life he had contemplated entering the priesthood. Father Vincent Damuah, for instance, had been one of his original Council members in January 1982. Rawlings' attitude to the hierarchy, however, remained ambivalent. Conflict with the Catholic hierarchy began to emerge from the middle of 1982 when the Catholic Bishops issued a communiqué strongly condemning certain aspects of 'the revolutionary process', in particular, the random assaults and killings which had so badly stained that year. In April 1983 the Bishop of Accra, the Right Reverend Dominic Andoh, ordered the Dutch missionary Father Joop Visser to withdraw from practising in his diocese. Father Visser was the priest in charge of Medina parish in Accra and the grounds for his removal were that he was too closely associated with the revolutionary process. He had spoken publicly on political platforms and made clear his disagreement with certain aspects of the Bishops' criticisms of the revolution. Father Visser was well-known to Rawlings who greatly admired his work and who felt that his dismissal was a deliberate attempt by the privileged hierarchy of the Church to undermine the people's revolution. This was followed in April 1985 by a similar case in which the Bishop of Kumasi, the Right Reverend Peter Sarpong, requested the withdrawal from his diocese of two further expatriate missionaries, Father Joop Valentin and Mr John Crawford. They were, from the Church's point of view, becoming too involved in lay political matters and neglecting their religious responsibilities.

The Catholic newspaper, the *Catholic Standard*, had for some time maintained a critical stance on the matter of the PNDC's record on human rights, focusing in particular on the continued detention without trial of a number of individuals. This, combined with several extremely critical editorials, was to lead to a ban on the paper by the end of the year, but in the meantime the withdrawal of the two expatriate missionaries in mid-1985 prompted Rawlings to let loose a tirade of personal abuse against the Bishop of Kumasi which was broadcast live on public radio.

In his defence Rawlings argues that his insulting public criticism of certain people of high standing is intended to demystify the élitism of that strata of society who appear to consider themselves in some way superior to the 'common man'. He is thus trying to raise the self-respect of the common man, by showing that one man does not have to be subservient to another just because the latter holds an apparently important position. While it may make for good entertainment, it does not make for good government. Through speaking in this manner, Rawlings unnecessarily antagonises some potential friends, including in many cases those who hold some empathy for his basic goals and principles; and in lowering respect for those who are held in public esteem, he undermines the concept of respect for authority per se. Ultimately, that includes the Head of State himself.

Rawlings sees part of his role as Head of State to be that of watch-dog for the people. As such he speaks his mind and intervenes whenever he sees what he considers an injustice, corruption or incompetence. In this role he is likely to turn up unannounced at a ministry, corporation office or public works and make a spot check on what is going on, especially if he has already heard of some irregularity.

In August 1983, for instance, Rawlings heard that the Ministry of Trade's Workers' Defence Committee had tried to shield two of its members who had been caught stealing trading licence books from their place of work. The executive committee of the WDC had apparently written to the local police station saying that they had already dealt with the matter internally and the case should therefore be dropped. When Rawlings heard of this, he immediately went to the police and told them to re-open the case. He then went on to the Ministry of Trade where he harangued the WDC for more than an hour on their responsibilities as participants in the decision-making process. The purpose of the revolution and the structure of the defence committees, he told them, was to give working people like themselves a share in the running of the country. This opportunity carried a heavy responsibility: their duty was to expose crime not to cover it up, no matter who was involved. Running a country like Ghana, he went on, was 'not the same as running a sentimental charity club!' It was a very complex business and every little part of it must be running smoothly in order for the whole to function properly and prosper. Rawlings seldom misses an opportunity to try to educate the people on what he perceives to be their responsibilities as citizens of the new Ghana.

The direct, hands-on approach of the Head of State extends even to the judicial system which, through the new Public Tribunals, Rawlings has tried to make more accessible to the ordinary Ghanaian. The Public Tribunals were introduced in 1982 to provide a quick and simple alternative to the complex and expensive traditional legal system which in the eyes of Rawlings – and the 'common man' – seemed more intent on employing lawyers and protecting the élites than serving ordinary people with simple justice. At the same time, Rawlings had learned from the way the independent judiciary of the Third Republic had contravened the constitution in overthrowing the decisions of the AFRC's Special Courts. Thus the Public Tribunal Law, PNDC Law 24, was structured in such a way that the Tribunals were ultimately answerable to the Council (the PNDC) and in effect, if he wanted to assert his authority, that meant Rawlings himself. In this way Rawlings is free to intervene if he considers that his concept of 'justice' is being contravened by the Tribunal courts. He does not often intervene, but he has done so on a number of notable occasions.

In August 1984 a man named Nii Amoo-Addy was tried by Public Tribunal on a charge of murder. The man's defence was that he had not intended to kill the victim whom he had shot at close range. The Tribunal acquitted him on the grounds that the accused was not familiar with the mechanism of the weapon that he used. Rawlings was furious when he heard the reason for the acquittal, especially as Amoo-Addy was his own nephew. As he saw it, the court's decision threatened to discredit the whole Tribunal system for being seen to favour the relatives of the Head of State. He ordered the immediate re-arrest of Amoo-Addy and called for the judgement papers. He then went on radio and television and publicly condemned the judgement in his characteristically forthright manner:

> The reasons for the verdict, as we have heard them, are absurd, an insult to the intelligence of the public. The Public Tribunal was established to represent the conscience of the people, not to insult them in this way. This can only destroy confidence in popular justice. Some of the tribunals are beginning to take on the characteristics of some of the traditional courts.

The case was re-heard before the Appeals Tribunal and the man was subsequently convicted and executed. The case illustrates the power which Rawlings has at his disposal, should he wish to exercise it. Rawlings' ability to intervene like this, of course, goes against the concept of independent justice as known and practised by the lawyers of the traditional legal system. For this reason most of the members of the Ghana Bar Association have boycotted the Public Tribunals, regarding them with some contempt as little more than an extension of the dictatorial power of the Ghanaian Head of State.

The Amoo-Addy case came at a time when Rawlings and the PNDC were making strenuous efforts to bring a greater degree of control over the arbitrary abuse of power by certain sectors of the security forces who for the past few years had been behaving at times as if their every word was law. In asserting this control Rawlings realised that if the revolution was ever to achieve the lasting credibility that he desired, then the exercise of power by the security forces which had brought the 31 December revolution into being, must be beyond reproach. Rawlings was acutely aware of the dangers of the arbitrary abuse of power and for this reason he came down even harder on friends and relatives who behaved as if they were above the law. The classic case was that of his long-time friend and Air Force contemporary Flight Lieutenant Larry Kojo Lee.

While on curfew patrol with two NCOs in the Accra suburb of Labadi on the evening of 28 October 1983, Flight Lieutenant Lee shot dead local resident Mr Peter Atsu Bieboo and left his body lying in the road. Neither of the NCOs who were with him, nor the Public Tribunal which tried Lee for murder a few weeks later, saw any valid reason for the shooting. In finding Lee guilty and condemning him to death by firing squad, the Chairman of the Tribunal remarked: 'The accused has a sentiment for reaching for his weapon over every little issue.' Lee indicated that he intended to petition the Chairman of the PNDC, as was his right under PNDC Law 24, and he let it be known that he expected clemency from his friend, the Head of State. Shortly afterwards, PNDC Law 74 introduced an appeals procedure to the tribunal courts and for most of 1984 Lee's case awaited a hearing before the new National Appeals Tribunal. At the end of September 1984 the Appeals Tribunal dismissed Lee's appeal on the technicality that the new law had come into force after Lee's original sentence had been passed. Lee's lawyer, Johnny Hansen, announced that his client's petition to the Chairman of the PNDC under Law 24 still stood, but Rawlings would not even consider a petition for clemency from his friend for to have done so would in his view have fatally undermined public respect for the law. Without even replying to the petition, he signed the death warrant and Lee was executed the following Saturday.

This sort of strong stand and ruthless determination to do whatever he considers right and just, is the kind of thing which makes Rawlings feared like an avenging angel. So what is it that wins him so much admiration? For, however much his critics may not like to admit it, Rawlings has a considerable popular following in the country at large, especially in the rural areas.

In the first place, of course, the PNDC has shifted the

power-base of the government away from the urban centres of southern Ghana and out into the rural areas. Under the PNDC farmers have been treated with more of the respect which they deserve and they have been paid far better for their crops than under any previous government.

In the second place, people believe in Rawlings' integrity and trust him to a far greater extent than they have most of his predecessors. From fear alone Ghanaians would never have followed him through the appallingly harsh times that they experienced in the early 1980s. Rawlings wins so many people's respect and trust partly through his down to earth approachability. He never considers himself above the common man or woman. Through his actions as well as words he frequently shows his immense respect for the hard-working farmers, especially the women of the remoter rural areas upon whom the country's native wealth ultimately depends.

By getting his hands dirty and working with the people, by putting out bush fires, carrying heavy sacks of maize and helping to dig out ditches, Rawlings does not appear to be seeking cheap publicity. By sleeping on a concrete floor covered only with a blanket, by camping on the Afram Plains and being bitten by mosquitoes, and then getting up at dawn to work upon some project, Rawlings is demonstrating the dignity of manual labour and the dignity of the living conditions of the poorest rural family. At the same time he is trying to narrow what he himself has termed 'the credibility gap' that exists between a person's words and his deeds. In his view, far too often past governments and politicians have made fine-sounding promises which were never followed through. Ministers passed off awkward questions about lack of concrete action with some clever manipulation of the facts. Rawlings, on the other hand, has striven to restore integrity to the word, and any Secretary of State who fails to follow through a commitment they have made will have to face the wrath of the Chairman.

Linked to the issue of the 'credibility gap' is Rawlings' appreciation of the importance of the human factor in the affairs of state. If something happens in the countryside, if there is a major accident or disaster, Rawlings immediately goes to the scene to express his sympathy and see if there is anything that he or the government can do to help. Thus he was furious when he learned, on returning to the country from an OAU conference in Addis Ababa in September 1985, that six days previously at the twin villages of Ekumfi Ekotsi and Bogyano a large private bus had ploughed through a procession of Akwambo Festival celebrants, killing twenty-six of them, and not a single member of government had thought to visit the bereaved. The morning after his return, Rawlings went to the site to express his sorrow and to hear from eye witnesses.

Where Secretaries of State may seek refuge in statistics which reassure them that things are going well, Rawlings is far more likely to be persuaded by the anecdotal evidence of the human factor. He has a powerful instinct which informs him whether things are right or wrong. Having made a judgement based partly upon this instinct, he takes a firm decision, acts swiftly upon it and it is difficult to persuade him to change his mind. Although leading to powerful and effective leadership, this characteristic of Rawlings' style of government also has its minus side. Thus one of his greatest personal faults is his preparedness to accept the truth of allegations about a colleague or opponent if his instinct tells him that the allegations fit the character of the person. In a country such as Ghana, long fertilised by rumour and strong on conspiracy theory, this can make for dangerous and unjust decisions, especially when it leads to sackings or detention without trial.

Notwithstanding the case of Larry Kojo Lee and others, a potentially damaging allegation levelled at Rawlings is that he has been soft on former friends who have fallen foul of the law, and that he has gathered around himself, as his closest advisers, people of his own Ewe 'tribe'. There is a careful distinction to be drawn here between balancing ethnic interests and practising 'tribalistic' preference. Like any politician of the past who believes in Ghanaian unity, Rawlings is aware of the need to show ethnic and regional balance in the affairs of government. For this reason, in January 1982, for instance, he was careful to emphasise the northern origins of many within the new PNDC government, for the 31 December revolution had just overthrown a northern President. The question of 'tribal' preference, however, is an altogether more explosive issue.

There is one particular instance in which Rawlings has laid himself open to accusations of special preference and that is what is known as 'the Quashigah affair'.

Captain Courage Quashigah played an important role in frustrating attempted coups against the PNDC in 1982 and 1983. He became the hero of the hour following the recapture of Broadcasting House on 19 June 1983. He received his regular promotion to Major and was later transferred from PNDC Headquarters to the Military Academy and although he was still seen as an important ally of the revolution, there were rumours that he was dissatisfied and felt he deserved greater recognition and promotion. Nevertheless, early in October 1989 the public were surprised to learn from an official announcement that Quashigah and four others had been arrested for plotting to assassinate the Head of State, J.J.Rawlings, the previous month. An investigation was held *in camera* and from the brief report that was released to the press in November 1989 it appeared that there was ample evidence to back up the allegations.

The peculiarity of the Quashigah case is the way that it has been handled in contrast to the normal way of treating those accused of plotting the overthrow of Rawlings. Normally, a suspected plotter is trailed by the Bureau of National Investigation. Evidence is accumulated, he is arrested, tried before a Public Tribunal and executed for treason. In Quashigah's case, his activities were known for some time. Rawlings had even suggested at one point that parental pressure be brought to bear to curb Quashigah's 'delusions of grandeur'! Finally, once he had been arrested and placed in detention, no further action was taken against him. At the time of writing, Quashigah is still in detention, without having been brought before a Public Tribunal.

Two critical points arise from this. On the one hand, Rawlings has been accused by human rights activists of detaining a man indefinitely without due trial. On the other hand, if he was brought to trial and the reputed evidence was valid, he would almost certainly face the firing squad. Given the alternatives of detention without trial or probable execution, is Quashigah receiving special treatment, and if so, why? Does Rawlings have one set of principles for his opponents and another for his friends? Past evidence would seem to suggest that this is generally not the case. Indeed, in the same context it is worth noting that investigations established the complicity of Victor Owusu in a previous coup plot. He was released from detention after a while and yet he is an Akan and not a friend of Rawlings. Until the Quashigah affair is ultimately resolved, however, the whole concept of preferential treatment will remain a weapon for critics of the PNDC to wield against the Chairman.

Finally, on the international scene, Rawlings rarely feels at ease in the council chambers and cocktail parties of the diplomatic circuit, perhaps because he sees through much of the hypocrisy that passes off as modern diplomacy. He is not a man for idle pleasantries and he has no patience with the evasiveness of diplomatic speech. Nevertheless, he regards the field of foreign affairs as a matter of the greatest importance to the future and integrity of Ghana; and it can be taken as significant that he has given special responsibility for foreign affairs to his most powerful political ally on the Council, Captain Kojo Tsikata. He maintains a careful watch on foreign affairs and more often than not provides the lead in decisions on Ghana's foreign policy.

The stance of Ghana under the PNDC has been principally one of non-alignment. Rawlings jealously guards the independence of Ghana and does not hesitate to speak out against what he perceives to be encroachment upon the territorial integrity of any member country of the Non-Aligned Movement. He has, of course, seen evidence of numerous attempts by the CIA to destabilise his own country and he is very watchful and suspicious of the motives and the actions of that most powerful of governments, the United States.

The countries with which Ghana under Rawlings has most closely identified have been Nicaragua under the Sandinistas and, until his untimely assassination, Burkina Faso under Captain Thomas Sankara. Ortega of Nicaragua and Sankara of Burkina Faso were people to whom Rawlings could easily relate. They were trying, like him, to bring about a genuine people's revolution and they were making giant strides in this direction in circumstances even more difficult than those existing in Ghana. Rawlings, and all the PNDC who met him, particularly admired the humility and integrity of Sankara, regarding him as an inspiration for their own revolution. What the Burkinabe were achieving under Sankara's leadership, never ceased to amaze those Ghanaians who were witness to it, and Sankara's death was a serious blow to the Ghanaian revolution. Rawlings' position on Libya, on the other hand, has been somewhat more ambivalent.

While numerous Third World leaders silently applauded the US raid on Tripoli in 1986, Rawlings saw it as an attack against the territorial integrity of every member of the Non-Aligned Movement. He accepted that many nations were opposed to Gaddafi and his Libyan people's revolution. Rawlings himself had his doubts about many things Gaddafi did, but he felt it was important to speak out in condemnation of the US action. In an interview on

Ghanaian television on 23 April 1986 Rawlings stated his position:

> The principles which bind the countries of the Non-Aligned Movement abhor acts of aggression such as the attack on Libya which undermines the independence of all our countries. What is happening to Libya is the larger version of what many of us have been suffering at the hands of the Reagan Administration. The attack could have been on any one of us. It is only logical therefore that we show solidarity with Libya in these trying moments.

Then, in words which typify Rawlings' personal style in foreign affairs, the Ghanaian leader went on to comment:

> . . . if the US wants to assume this position of power over the rest of the world, then we should all have a say in who gets sent to the White House.
>
> The USA seems to need help in order to understand the reality of international affairs.

Rawlings was thus consistent in his thinking when on the occasion of the Gulf crisis he roundly condemned Saddam Hussein for being so foolish as to invade Kuwait. It was not so much for his violent resolution of a territorial dispute that he condemned Saddam, but rather for his betrayal of Third World independence by playing into the hands of the United States and allowing the US government the opportunity to take unto itself the right to intervene in world affairs wherever it saw fit.

In making his opening address at a conference of the Non-Aligned Movement's foreign ministers in Accra in September 1991, Chairman Rawlings returned to the theme of the Gulf crisis and warned the delegates of the 103 countries present: 'We must not let conflicts between member countries degenerate into a situation which others can exploit to serve their own ends.'

It was the first high-level meeting of the Non-Aligned Movement since the ending of the Cold War and many foreign ministers at the conference felt that the concept of non-alignment was no longer relevant. Rawlings, on the other hand, took the view that in the light of the current 'superpower monopoly' of the United States government and the increasing polarisation of the nations of the world into rich and poor, groupings such as the Non-Aligned Movement must learn to work even more closely together in order to promote the interests of the Third World.

Chapter 7

The Evolving Democratic Process

On 31 December 1981 Rawlings committed his incoming government to the establishment of an entirely new and effective system of 'popular democracy'. It was presented as the basic rationale for seizing power from the elected government of the Third Republic. The phrases 'participation in the decision-making process' and 'people's participatory democracy' became catch-phrases of the revolution which set itself the task of reshaping Ghanaian society.

As we saw in Chapter Four, this was to be achieved through the spontaneous establishment of popular defence committees. Through the PDCs and WDCs of 1982 and 1983 many ordinary Ghanaians who had never previously participated in any decision-making process outside their immediate family did indeed assume some degree of local power in the work-place and in the residential community. It was not, however, the sort of participatory democracy which many in the PNDC had envisaged. Perhaps part of the problem was that Rawlings, in particular, had not clearly thought through the practical implementation of this kind of people's power. He had accepted the formulations presented to him by the intellectuals of the JFM and other influential left-wing groupings and he assumed that it would work in Ghana as it seemed to have done in Libya, Cuba and Nicaragua.

Once the process started, however, those who formed the defence committees proceeded, from Rawlings' point of view, to take *too much* part in the decision-making process. Their decisions were often ill-informed, hasty and sometimes downright disastrous. The power they wielded seemed arbitrary in nature. The executive committees of some of the PDCs became a law unto themselves and were perceived by many of those whom they were supposed to represent as little more than the bully-boys of the Rawlings' revolution.

By the middle of 1982 Rawlings could perceive that the people's power which his revolution had unleashed was in danger of verging on anarchy. To a man of his military and highly-disciplined mind, this was a situation which needed more control from the centre. The defence committees, however, had their champions in the left-wing of the JFM who, by the second half of 1982, were finding themselves at odds with Rawlings in the central councils of government. For a while, the future of the defence committees became entangled in ideological disputes within the PNDC.

Gradually, during 1983 and 1984 the PDCs and WDCs were brought under some greater degree of control; their functions were codified, an authority structure was established and in November 1984 they were redefined as Committees for the Defence of the Revolution (CDRs), answerable ultimately to a Secretary of State. They thus became, in effect, the functionaries of a ministry. Their purpose was now to initiate local development projects, organise voluntary labour for community works, present problems and complaints to government and arbitrate in local civil disputes. The important change that had taken place in November 1984 was the weakening of that element of local independent political power which had characterised the PDCs in the early days of the revolution. The CDRs retained the important role of responsibility for political education, but from now on it was more as a conduit for interpreting government directives and explaining to the masses 'the aims of the revolution', as defined by central government. They were, in effect, now a wing of the PNDC.

The CDRs, like their predecessor PDCs, were primarily organisations run by men. Parallel to the evolution of the CDRs, however, was a voluntary organisation similar in objective, but totally different in composition. It was an organisation exclusively for women. It was known as the 31 December Women's Movement and in some ways it has become even more powerful than the CDRs themselves.

The 31 December Women's Movement was founded on 15 May 1982, the third anniversary of Rawlings' first appearance on the Ghanaian national stage. It was founded by a small group of women who were keen to ensure that women in general did not get left behind in the rapidly evolving revolutionary process of 1982. It was founded to mobilise women's initiative: to awaken them politically in support of the revolution, to promote and protect the interests of women in the new society and to get women themselves looking after their own interests. The name of the organisation clearly stated its orientation and the founding executive committee was able to play its trump card by persuading Mrs Nana Konadu Agyeman Rawlings to become the President of the movement.

Women are the bedrock of Ghanaian life. They work extremely hard, far harder than most Ghanaian men, and often for very little reward. They work not only in the home, in child-care and in looking after and supporting their husbands, but they also work upon the land. In the rural areas they produce most of the food that feeds the family and almost everywhere they engage in trade. Although they are economically very active, women, hitherto, had not been very organised as a group. Individual women may have been very vocal, but they seldom got themselves heard. The founders of the 31 December Women's Movement realised the need to make women stronger and better organised in Ghanaian society, not to compete with men, but to stand on their own two feet. There was above all the issue of 'participatory democracy'. So far the male-dominated defence committees had taken all the initiative in the new decision-making process. Why should women, who make up 51 per cent of Ghanaian society, sit and watch the other 49 per cent make all the decisions?

It was realised from the beginning that if women were to stand on their own feet and take a fair share of the new participatory democracy, they would need economic as well as social and political development. They must have some degree of financial independence. This organisation was to be based on actions, not high-sounding words. Women needed day-care centres to help look after their children while they were working on their farms, selling their produce or attending meetings and mobilising women in support of the new movement. In order to pay for these, they would need income-generating projects, for they did not wish to turn to the state for financial help. That was not the purpose of having Mrs Rawlings as their President. Women needed to *prove* that they could stand on their own.

The growth of the organisation was slow in the first year, but in 1983 Mrs Rawlings went to Cuba where she saw at first hand the extent and the depth of women's organisation throughout even the remotest rural areas. When she reported back to Ghana, the movement started to set up a network of branches in every region of the country. In due course, an inter-connecting network of 31 December Women's committees was established in every district capital and from there they moved out into the villages. The aim was to take the initiative to the countryside, where the need was felt to be greatest, and not to leave the organisation dependent upon the executive committee in Accra.

It was easy enough to set up branches in the rural areas because they used the established network of traditional society. In every town and tiny village there is a queen mother or prominent lady who is the traditional source of advice for women's marital, family or social problems. The 31 December Women went to the queen mothers first and explained their objectives and ideals. Once she was persuaded of the movement's value, she called in the women of the village for discussion. In this way a new branch of the movement could quickly get started, everybody in the village would know what it was all about and, with approval from the queen mother, it was usually readily supported. If, for some reason, the queen mother refused her support, then it was hard to get a branch established.

The basic principle of the movement was that each and every branch of the organisation must be responsible for initiating its own projects, according to the particular local needs. With the assistance of queen mothers, the traditional authorities could be persuaded to make land available and many of the rural projects were based initially upon small communal farms. The women of the movement would grow crops on the land, such as cassava, make it into garri and sell it in the town. The money raised would either go into further income-generating projects, or be put directly into some social scheme. Thus a small cassava farm, poultry unit or piggery might finance a day-care centre or a village well. Where the CDRs tended to expect money from central government for building toilets or digging drains, the women generated their own money, all of which, apart from running costs, was fed back into further projects.

Even the head office in Accra was financed by its own income-generating projects. It started with a *kenkey* factory which became so financially successful that it in turn provided the capital to set up a bakery. In due course, money raised from both these projects was put into establishing day-care centres in Accra.

By early 1991 the 31 December Women's Movement was financing 500 day-care centres throughout the whole country. The movement's success in developing social facilities such as these attracted the attention of international agencies, including some from the United Nations, which have provided small amounts of capital for the eradication of guinea-worm and for digging wells. Similarly, the Japanese have provided money for food processing, grain storage and irrigation projects. When PAMSCAD came into operation, the movement was able to initiate projects for that as well and it was through PAMSCAD that the 31 December Women's Movement indirectly began to get some financial help from government. At the same time they get help from the personnel of various ministries.

The 31 December Women's Movement is far more than just a facilitating organisation for social welfare projects. It is perceived by many as primarily a political organisation and there are ample grounds for this interpretation. It was founded quite deliberately to promote the ideals and objectives of the 31 December revolution and it still retains this highly political flavour which associates it strongly with the government of the PNDC. The high profile of the movement's President lends it the authority of a quasi-governmental organisation, even it if is, strictly speaking, independent. On her visits to the rural areas Mrs Rawlings receives the assistance and hospitality of Chiefs and Regional Secretaries, all of which helps the organisation in its many worthy projects. The attention given to Mrs Rawlings is no more than that due to the First Lady of the country and government assistance to the movement can be portrayed as recognition of the value of its voluntary social work; but it would be naïve not to recognise that the government itself regards the 31 December Women's Movement as an important source of political support for the PNDC and its policies.

From a small initial membership in 1982, the movement has grown rapidly since the mid-1980s so that by the end of 1990 it could claim three-quarters of a million registered members, with an associate membership of probably double that number. Many smaller women's groups have found it both useful and politic to join the 31 December Women's umbrella. This is partly a recognition of the movement's social and economic success. It is also a recognition of its political influence.

In the absence of legalised political parties under the rule of the PNDC, the 31 December Women's Movement has paralleled the CDRs as the nearest thing to a legal political party in Ghana since 1982. The perception of the movement as the political wing of the PNDC has brought it opponents as well as supporters. In some cases women have deliberately avoided the movement because of its clear links with 31 December and with the Rawlings name. They have feared that if Rawlings were overthrown, they might face arrest or harassment as part of his regime. In time, as the practical benefits have emerged, many of these initial fears have waned. Nevertheless, the 31 December Women's Movement is still widely feared as a very powerful organisation. It is believed that through the organisation and its President, members can gain the ear of the Head of State. Petitions and appeals against injustice are referred to Mrs Rawlings in the sure knowledge that if the case is strong enough, and the allegations of injustice or corruption firmly founded, the details will be passed on to her husband. Then woe betide the wrong-doer as the Head of State, with his customary vigour, activates the full process of the law. Similarly, it is feared that the converse is also true and that the 31 December Women's Movement is the eyes and ears of the Head of State.

The sharpest critics of the movement remain the intellectual women of the cities who view its political orientation with suspicion. They themselves do not feel the need for a social and economic self-help organisation, and, unaccustomed as they are to seeing the wife of their Head of State so active in public life, many look with scorn upon her activities to help the poor, assuming it must be purely politically motivated. Perhaps some would feel more at ease if the First Lady devoted her energies to shopping sprees in Europe, rather than promoting women's production in the rural areas!

On a national scale the 31 December Women's Movement has acted as an effective pressure group in ways that have benefited all the women of Ghana, no matter what their social or economic background. Thus it was a combination of the 31 December Women's Movement, the National Council for Women in Development and the Ghana branch of the Federation of International Women Lawyers which, in 1985, pushed the PNDC into enacting a key set of laws affecting the lives of women. The new laws cover the fields of family accountability, intestate succession, administration of estates and customary marriage and divorce. Taken together, they have been an important step towards assuring the women of Ghana equality of treatment before the law.

The CDRs and the 31 December Women's Movement together may have brought the ordinary men and women of Ghana much more directly into the decision-making process on certain local issues and awoken their political consciousness; but if there was ever to be a properly constituted form of 'participatory democracy', then some other more formal structure would have to be evolved.

In 1982, in one of its first proclamations, the PNDC had announced the setting up of a National Commission for Democracy (NCD). Hitherto, its equivalent in the Third Republic, the Electoral Commission, had confined its responsibilities to the electoral side of parliamentary democracy: the drawing up of an electoral register and the supervision of elections. The responsibilities of the NCD, by contrast, were to extend far beyond the 'empty token' of the ballot box. It was to become in itself an essential part of the democratic process. While the PDC structure was still being considered as the appropriate route towards the new democracy, however, the NCD remained little more than an idea on paper. In those early years of the revolution all the energies of government were focused on resolving the acute economic crisis. In the words of a Ghanaian saying, quoted by Justice D.F.Annan: 'It's only when your belly is full that you can whistle, for nobody whistles on an empty stomach.' It was thus not until 1984, at a time when the PDCs were being transformed into the CDRs and the economic recovery programme had begun to show results that attention was once more turned towards the NCD.

PNDC Law 42 defined the principal functions of the NCD as threefold. Firstly, it was to engage in political education. Hitherto Ghanaian politics had been dominated by personalities rather than policies. The NCD was to change all this by stimulating political discussion at all levels of society. Secondly, the NCD was to advise the government on how obstacles to a true democracy could best be removed. Finally, a very important function of the Commission was to monitor interaction between the people and the government and assess to what extent the government of the day was carrying out the people's wishes.

In July 1984 Justice Daniel F. Annan was appointed the first Chairman of the NCD and by September 1984 the rest of the membership had been constituted. The initial membership comprised the technocrats of the former Electoral Commission, combined with selected political appointees from the Committee of Secretaries, academics and representatives of workers through the TUC and the CDRs. It was a disparate grouping, representing almost as many political tendencies as there were members and much of its first eighteen months of meetings was taken up by theoretical wrangling over the ideology of the new democracy. It was not until early in 1986 that political consensus was reached and the NCD began functioning properly according to its constitution. Much of the credit for its survival as a coherent body during this early period must go to Justice Annan whose dogged persistence pulled the Commission through in one piece.

During 1986 and early 1987 the NCD held a number of political seminars in the various regional capitals to discuss the type of democracy which should be evolved for the future. By the middle of 1987 the members of the Commission felt it was ready to submit its first report to the PNDC on how best to institutionalise a form of participatory democracy. The report, popularly known as 'The Blue Book', was published in July 1987. It proposed a system for elected local assemblies which would enable the maximum number of people to participate in the kinds of decisions which affected their day to day life.

The Blue Book was referred to another session of regional seminars to try the ideas out on a wide range of people. These were conducted before invited audiences in every regional capital where the main concerns seemed to be residential qualifications and the minimum age for voting. The question of residence was crucial for although many people lived and worked for most of their lives in the big cities like Accra, they considered their 'home' to be the village where their family came from. Should they register as residents in city or in village? In the end a flexible system was evolved whereby a person could choose his or her official residence for voting purposes. The voting age was finally fixed at eighteen. The NCD also commissioned a number of written reports on the proposals from academics and professionals whose opinion they valued in the field of local democracy. In addition, numerous unsolicited papers were submitted to the Commission at various stages of the evolving process, some critical, most of them constructive.

The strongest critics of the whole idea contained within the Blue Book tended to hold aloof from the NCD, regarding it as little more than a cypher for the arbitrary wishes of the PNDC, of which Justice Annan was a member. Indeed

Justice Annan's membership of the Council has been regularly used by some of the government's most eloquent opponents as proof that the NCD was not an independent body and therefore the PNDC could not be genuinely interested in democracy. The one does not necessarily follow from the other. So far as the PNDC is concerned, the NCD was never intended to be a totally independent body. It was a creation of the revolution and its work must, therefore, be expected to reflect the general aims of the revolution. That is not to say that it is prevented by definition from coming up with its own, clear and reasoned set of proposals, but simply that they must fall within the general political parameters of 'participatory democracy'.

From July 1987 to the middle of 1988 the NCD was simultaneously engaged in drawing up a comprehensive voters' register. It was quickly realised that if there was to be a genuinely representative local assembly, then the number of administrative districts would have to be increased from 65 to 110. By the end of October 1988 the preparations were complete and the government published PNDC Law 207, setting out the structure and functions of the new system for elected district government.

The District Assembly was to be the highest political and administrative authority in the district. It was supposed to 'guide, supervise, administer and control' all other political and administrative authorities in the district. It would have the power to raise local finances from specified sources, such as levies on individuals, on entertainment and on trade. It would initiate development projects and ultimately, when central government departments were decentralised to the districts, it would have more or less full control over those departments that most affected them, especially health and education.

A notable feature that distinguished the new system of District Assemblies from previous forms of local government was the fact that election to the assembly was to be on a non-partisan basis. All political parties had been banned in January 1982 and they were not about to be revived in 1988. It was strongly felt by the NCD that one of the major problems of previous electoral systems, even at local government level, was their domination by remote party élites who, from their headquarters in the city, chose the candidates themselves and then ensured their election by the amount of money spent on party propaganda. The new system of non-partisan, independent candidates would ensure that each electoral area would be able to choose and elect a local person to represent them in the local assembly.

The NCD supervised every stage of the elections, but the electoral task was so huge and some of the districts so remote that the whole process had to be staggered over several months. The country was divided into three zones and the election was completed in one zone before moving on to the next. Voting started in November 1988 and was not completed until the end of February 1989. In each of the 4840 electoral areas a maximum of five candidates was allowed to stand. Campaigning was restricted to two or three weeks. The concern was to ensure that wealthy candidates had no particular advantage over any of their opponents, so no public rallies were allowed, posters with symbols and slogans were banned and leaflets, paid for by the NCD, were restricted to a single sheet containing biographical notes about the candidate. Some managed to improve on this by adding a photograph showing themselves in suit and tie.

One of the most controversial aspects of the electoral process was the common platform. On a certain selected day shortly before the vote, all the candidates in each electoral area were required to share a public platform to answer any questions that might be put to them by the electorate. This was to guard against the empty electoral promises which had characterised previous elections. It was very popular in the rural areas as most of the candidates were well-known locally and, on numerous occasions, candidates were embarrassed by awkward questions about their personal integrity. Some even had their past misdeeds 'exposed' and were shamed into stepping down.

Most of the candidates were teachers and farmers and, although few were women, when it came to voting day, as many as two-thirds of the votes were cast by women. This pattern of predominantly women voting could be traced to a number of factors. It has been said by some that perhaps it stems from the role of women in traditional Ghanaian society: women, through the queen mothers, are the 'king-makers' and their turning out to vote in such large numbers for predominantly male candidates may have been symbolic of their traditional behind the scenes role. On the other hand, the politicisation of women for electoral purposes has historical roots in the 1950s when Nkrumah mobilised the women of Ghana as a bedrock of support for the CPP. Probably more significant than either of these, however, has been the success of the 31 December Women's Movement in raising the consciousness of women about national and political affairs.

The NCD estimated that it managed to register 80 per cent of the potential voters in the country and that 59 per cent of these actually voted: that is, just under 50 per cent of the total potential electorate, whereas in 1979 the number of people who voted was barely 35 per cent of registered voters. So the figure for the District Assemblies showed a considerable advance of interest over previous national elections. The place where the elections were least supported was in the large metropolitan areas, especially Accra, where people generally have a less-developed sense of local collective responsibility. It is also true that most of the open opposition to the PNDC in general, and the new District Assembly concept in particular, came from the former party politicians of the urban areas.

The District Assembly concept has come in for a good

deal of criticism from opponents of the PNDC. Certain people baulk particularly at its non-partisan character which they see as a deliberate attempt to exclude them from local politics. By way of protest, many of the professional and business classes boycotted the elections, denigrating them as a recipe for government by the illiterate and the CDRs. The second principal objection has been that only two-thirds of each assembly is actually elected, the rest being appointees of central government, acting on varied local advice. Taken together with the fact that the PNDC District Secretary is an *ex officio* member of the assembly and Chairman of its Executive Committee, this is seen by many as an extension of authoritarian control by an unelected central government.

In fact, historically, the concept of an appointed minority is nothing new in Ghanaian local politics. In practice, the appointed members of the assemblies have been anything but government stooges and, except on very rare occasions, they have not formed the sort of anti-democratic block which their critics had predicted. They include Chiefs, Churchmen and people of various professions considered useful in local government but which are under-represented among the elected members. In a few instances the appointees have even included some well-known critics of the PNDC. On the issue of the District Secretary's role, while central government still retains responsibility for national development issues, it is only logical that some sort of supervisory eye be kept on District Assembly initiatives to see that they co-ordinate with regional and national plans. The District Assemblies could undoubtedly be more democratic and be freer to act more independently of central government. However, this is seen by the PNDC as something that can develop with greater political experience at the local level combined with greater decentralisation and the delegation of more administrative functions to the districts.

The quality of District Assemblies varies enormously.

Experience has shown that a District Assembly in an area where there is a serious chieftaincy dispute is unlikely to achieve very much because the local community is divided and the necessary consensus on priorities is difficult to achieve. Some District Assembly members attempt to lord it over the community they are supposed to represent, unnecessarily antagonising the local chief and elders and imposing unreasonable restrictions or charges on the local population. The best of them, however, have been vibrant and useful centres of local accountability in government. They have initiated important local projects, such as repair of school buildings, health centres, feeder roads or market centres. For these projects they are required to raise half the money locally before appealing to central government for the balance. This in itself has awoken a sense of local civic responsibility within the districts which had been conspicuously absent in the past. The Ministry of Local Government plays a co-ordinating role with the relevant ministry.

Some of the Assembly members place personal expenses high on the list of priorities and in a few of the districts the amount of money devoted to expenses far exceeds that spent on specific projects. Nevertheless, it is the beginning of a process of evolution. The Assembly members have learned that they have a voice which is heard and is reported in the state-owned press, even when it is critical of central government. Their presence in the districts, especially under the PNDC which is so anxious to prove its democratic credentials, has begun to make genuine decentralisation and local accountability not only a possibility, but also a reality.

As the District Assemblies approach the end of their first three-year term of office, any reasonable assessment of them must admit that they have confounded many of their critics and that they have on the whole laid a successful foundation for the further evolution of democratic government at district level.

The PNDC had always recognised that the establishment of District Assemblies was only the first step in a move towards a democratic structure for central government; but just as the PNDC had made its first priority achieving democracy at local level, so it was determined that its future evolution to national level should be developed from that district base. The logical route was to establish Regional Assemblies, possibly drawn from the membership of the District Assemblies, which would co-ordinate development projects on a regional scale. A National Assembly would be the last to evolve. Clearly, a broad time-scale would be necessary if one was to develop from the other; but then the PNDC was in no hurry to abdicate power until the evolution of a form of popular democracy which would ensure long-term stability and the continuity of that social and economic development which it as a government had struggled so hard to achieve.

Rawlings spelt out the PNDC position in a national broadcast in March 1989, just after the completion of the District Assembly elections: 'It is not for a handful of people in Accra to say when and how, or even if, regional and national assemblies should be established.' The District Assemblies, he said, should be able to formulate guidelines for subsequent stages of government based on their experiences. 'The ultimate task of the PNDC is to make itself redundant, but not by artificially conceived or borrowed forms of government.' He believed some new form of stable Ghanaian democracy could be evolved 'by trusting the good sense of the people to arrive at an appropriate system.' This of course was deliberately vague and destined to take place at some unspecified time in the future.

Once the prospect of a national constitutional democracy had been re-opened, however, it was impossible simply to allow it to evolve over a long period of time. Too long had already been allowed to elapse since the declaration of 31 December 1981 which stated that nothing would be done from the Castle 'without the consent and the authority of the people.' Security problems and an economic crisis had intervened, but if the PNDC wanted to retain the initiative, then it had to act swiftly. As soon as the District Assemblies had got under way, the National Commission for Democracy turned its attention to the next stage in the evolutionary process. It was soon realised that the prospect of an intermediate Regional Assembly was fraught with problems, in particular the danger of its promotion of regional ethnic rivalries – that scourge of so much of modern Africa's national unity. Although the prospect of regional co-ordinating authorities was still not ruled out, it became clear from the beginning that the main focus of future debate would be on a constitution for government at national level.

The NCD followed its usual course of conducting regional seminars. The first of these was held in Sunyani, the capital of Brong-Ahafo Region, on 5 July 1990. A notable characteristic of these ten regional fora, held between July and November 1990, was that, unlike their predecessors of 1986, 1987 and 1988, they attracted considerable attention and controversy throughout the country.

Government at local level had not been perceived as particularly important in Ghana in the past. Government since independence had been a highly centralised affair. Accra was where the real power lay and to the majority of Ghanaians any discussion of a constitution meant central government, politicians and national elections. The PNDC itself had been a highly centralised government for most of its period in office. It had also been a particularly powerful and determined government, brooking no opposition or serious criticism of its fundamental revolutionary objectives. With the suspension of the Habeas Corpus Act and the widespread use of arbitrary detention, critics had for years been cowed or suppressed into silent acquiescence. Now, suddenly, the PNDC seemed about to open up discussion on the evolution of a democratic structure for central government. It was the first sign for nearly a decade that the

Provisional National Defence Council was seriously considering its own 'Provisional' nature.

The *People's Daily Graphic,* in describing the forum at Sunyani, referred to it as the first in a series of seminars for Assembly men and women, District Secretaries and CDRs and that is what it appeared to be. Vocal critics, especially aspirant national politicians, maintained that the fora in themselves were far from democratic in their conduct or their composition: they were rigged by government to simulate open debate and this gave the lie to the PNDC's declared democratic intentions.

It is true that as many as two-thirds of the members present at the fora were invited; but, the NCD argued, this was because it was anxious to ensure that they should be as representative as possible of the local community that they served. They were not simply seminars *in the regional capital,* but seminars *for the people of the region.* The clearest and most democratically-chosen representatives of each local district were the District Assemblies, so delegates from each Assembly were invited. Similarly delegates from the CDRs and 31 December Women's Movement were invited as representatives of a large number of local people. In addition, the NCD invited chiefs and elders and representatives from a broad cross-section of recognised identifiable bodies, which included teachers, nurses, farmers and trade unionists. One of the fora's most vocal critics, the Ghana Bar Association, was conspicuous by its refusal to attend. They seemed to regard the whole affair as a farce: little more than a meeting of the PNDC with its sycophantic supporters. Perhaps they were resentful of the government's deliberate side-lining of that class of legal experts which had dominated the drafting of Ghana's previous constitutions.

The opening session was attended by Chairman Rawlings, Justice Annan and key members of the government, such as the Secretaries for Information and Local Government. Formal speeches were made by the Chairman and other dignitaries and specially-commissioned keynote papers were read before the matter was thrown open to the floor for debate. The overall theme for the series of fora was 'The District Assemblies and the Evolving Democratic Process'. It was clear that priority of consideration was being given to the role of the District Assemblies in any future democratic constitution.

Debate was highly stilted in the first forum at Sunyani. Later fora were more relaxed and when they got to Kumasi a number of individuals were quite outspoken in their calls for the resignation of the PNDC and the immediate lifting of the ban on political parties. In most of the fora, however, especially the early ones, discussion from the floor was dominated by District Assembly members who seemed to see this as their chance to preserve the power which they had so recently gained. They feared that in a national constitution they would be side-tracked; that government would once more pass into the hands of urban party élites and their role in participatory democracy would rapidly be undermined. The District Assembly delegates proposed that they, as the closest representatives of the people at local level, should form an electoral college and send members from among their own ranks to sit in the National Assembly in Accra. It was their opportunity to convert themselves into national politicians. Those Assembly members who accepted that separate national elections would be necessary, generally proposed that elections be conducted on the same sort of non-party basis which had enabled ordinary, inexperienced men and women like themselves to be elected at the local district level.

This dual theme of electoral college or non-party national elections was taken up by District Assembly-men and CDR representatives at each of the regional fora, to the extent that it was assumed by critics that they must have been primed by their District Secretaries and were therefore reflecting official PNDC policy. It seems more likely that they did not need any prompting. The fora were relayed country-wide on radio and television and Assembly members were acting out of a collective sense of self-preservation. It is also interesting to note that District Assembly delegates seemed well aware of the current world-wide moves towards political pluralism, in Africa as well as in Eastern Europe. A significant number of them were politically mature enough to observe that it may not be wise for Ghanaians to swim too strongly against the tide.

The opening of the Sunyani forum acted like a signal for the aspirant politicians of the impending Fourth Republic. Seeing that the future of national politics was now at last on the political agenda, and inspired perhaps by the euphoria of 'democracy' that appeared to be sweeping the world, they determined to seize the political initiative from the hands of the PNDC.

A few weeks after the Sunyani forum opponents of the PNDC began holding meetings of their own to try to wrest the discussion of a future constitution away from the hands of government. Leading members of the Kwame Nkrumah Revolutionary Guard (KNRG) held a press conference in which they took the line of 'liberal democracy', calling for a lifting of the 1982 ban on political parties, the release of all political prisoners and the setting up of a constituent assembly, as had been done in 1969 and 1979, to draw up and promulgate a new constitution. The KNRG had been formed as the Nkrumahist wing of the PNP, but following the revolution they had initially supported the PNDC. One of their leading members, Johnny Hansen, had been Secretary for the Interior in 1982–83. Hansen, however, had long ago fallen out with the PNDC and felt that the Rawlings' government had travelled too far in the pocket of the IMF. Now Hansen and other members of the KNRG, such as the freelance journalist Kwesi Pratt, helped to bring together an alliance of 'democrats' opposed to the PNDC and its perceived attempts to push through its own version of a democratic constitution.

On 1 August 1990 a loose alliance of former political groupings came together to launch an umbrella pressure group called the Movement for Freedom and Justice (MFJ). It was chaired by the eminent historian Professor Adu Boahen and prominent on its executive committee were lawyers Johnny Hansen, Ray Kakraba Quarshie and Obeng Manu. Affiliated to it were all the former political groupings of the First, Second and Third Republics whose party machinery had quietly lain under dust sheets for the duration of the PNDC regime. With membership crossing the great UP/CPP divide of Ghanaian politics, the founders of the MFJ obviously had a potentially powerful pressure group. The fact that the only thing many of them had in common was their desire to see a return to party politics and the resignation of the PNDC seemed not to matter for the moment. It was accepted among affiliates that the MFJ was a temporary marriage of convenience. They likened Rawlings' attempt to 'finesse a constitutional legitimacy' to that of Acheampong's ill-fated UNIGOV experiment of 1977–78. Like the similarly named People's Movement for Freedom and Justice of 1978, the MFJ of 1990 hoped to build up a whirlwind of momentum which would steal the initiative from the PNDC, force through a change to multi-party politics on the old pattern and ultimately bring about the collapse of Rawlings' government.

Jerry Rawlings, however, was no Kutu Acheampong and his record of eight-and-a-half years of relatively efficient, responsible and incorrupt government counted for considerably more than anything the SMC had ever produced. Rawlings, unlike the SMC I or II, could count not only on the loyal support of the military rank and file, but also on the wide support of people in the rural areas who appreciated the benefits of PNDC rule and distrusted the old style of professional politicians who had done so little for them in the past. In addition, Rawlings had working for him in the PNDC government a number of the former student leaders and other political activists who had cut their political teeth on the anti-UNIGOV movement of the late 1970s. They were not about to make the same sort of tactical errors which had helped to topple Acheampong.

While the PNDC proceeded with its fora, admittedly adopting a slightly more relaxed attitude towards open debate, it kept a tight grip on the activities of the MFJ, refusing it official recognition at the fora and depriving it of the oxygen of publicity. The MFJ meanwhile extended its umbrella to include the varied political organisations of the exiled community in Britain, such as those of Boakye Djan, J.H.Mensah and de Graft Johnson, all of whom looked forward to imminent repatriation to multi-party freedom in their home country. Despite the activities of the MFJ and the increasingly public demands from other quarters for an ending of detention without trial and greater personal freedom of expression, by the end of the year the PNDC still held the political initiative.

In an important keynote address to the nation, marking the ninth anniversary of the revolution and the beginning of the New Year, Chairman Rawlings laid out a political programme for 1991. The NCD would produce a report based on the recent regional fora, laying out its recommendations for 'the way forward', and present it to the PNDC by the end of March. A 'Consultative Assembly' would then be set up to make specific proposals for a new constitution by the end of 1991. He warned, however:

> We will proceed according to our Ghanaian pace and not upon the dictates of those who peddle models and abstract prescriptions without paying attention to specific circumstances ... [The new constitution] will derive from our historical experience and also from the democratic process set in motion on June 4th, 1979 and 31 December 1981.

Rawlings realised that Ghana was entering a critical new phase in her political history and the issue which concerned him more than any other was the spectre of conflict and the undoing of all that had been achieved, politically and economically, as he loosened the reins of power. In a heartfelt appeal to the nation Rawlings called for the restoration of trust and mutual understanding, and in this he was appealing as much to those inside Ghana as to the political exiles of the past decade whom he wished to see return:

> My dear countrymen and women, the time has come for us to show mutual trust and tolerance. We may not be particularly fond of each other but we need to be particularly tolerant of each other.
>
> Fellow Ghanaians, we stand at a crucial stage in our nation's history, conscious of the destiny that beckons to us all. We must hold out a hand of reconciliation, of trust and confidence. The hand must be open to all who seek the future well-being of our nation.
>
> I am not asking of anyone to abandon his interests; nor am I asking for anyone to suppress his opinions. I am simply and deeply convinced of the need for harmony and co-operation, of a common vision, common objectives and, above all, for the unity of our nation. Let us embrace the spirit of the times we live in whilst realising the spiritual values of our noble heritage.

The NCD was expected by its critics to echo the sentiments of the District Assembly members at the public fora and recommend to government a non-party political system, a sort of UNIGOV Mark II. The Commission, and with it the PNDC, therefore, surprised its critics and gained considerable credibility for its constitutional plans when its report, published at the end of March 1991, recommended the adoption of a multi-party system. It highlighted the uneasiness with which speakers at the fora had regarded the political parties of the past, but the NCD had been taking further political opinion, verbally and in writing and it concluded that some form of better controlled multi-party system for a National Assembly was what seemed best to satisfy the aspirations of a majority of Ghanaians.

The leaders of the MFJ appeared for a moment to be caught off guard, knowing, as they did, Rawlings' personal antipathy towards the party political system of the past. Their sense that they were somehow being finessed was heightened when in April the PNDC published its official reaction to the report. The PNDC accepted its recommendations and proposed to submit it to the Consultative Assembly as one of the major source documents for its deliberation. In the meantime, a special Committee of constitutional experts, under the chairmanship of Dr S.K.B. Asante, a former Solicitor-General, was set up to formulate by the end of July 1991 specific constitutional proposals, embodying the concerns of the NCD report, which would similarly be placed before the Consultative Assembly.

Matters were proceeding apace according to schedule, and the MFJ seemed unable to gain the moral high ground. It had been joined in its public utterances by a wide range of recognised bodies, including the Churches, the TUC and the Bar Association, all of which called for an immediate lifting of the ban on political parties, the ending of detention without trial, restoration of the Habeas Corpus Act and abolition of the laws requiring the registration of newspapers and of Churches – regarded as a restriction on the basic human freedoms of speech and religion. The focus of political attention now, however, had shifted to the composition of the Consultative Assembly and whether it should not rather be a Constituent Assembly with powers to promulgate its own constitution. Even the MFJ was now following the agenda set by the PNDC.

When the modalities for the Consultative Assembly were published in May 1991, lawyers, journalists and university students were outraged to learn that their opinions were to be given no more weight in the drafting of a constitution than those of traditional healers, bakers, hairdressers or canoe fishermen. Each recognised professional body or association of workers was allowed to send just one representative to the Consultative Assembly. Objectors to the presence of ten representatives from the National Council for Women in Development seemed to overlook the point that more than half the population of Ghana were women. In fact, by any comparison with previous constituent assemblies the one proposed by the PNDC was far more representative of the whole nation than those of 1968/69 and 1978/79.

At the time of this controversy the problem was put very well in a series of thoughtful editorials by Christian Aggrey, editor of the *Ghanaian Times*:

> The basic drive of the process towards constitutional rule is to ensure that the constitution that will finally emerge has the endorsement of the great majority of Ghanaians. All the leadership aspirants ... declare support for such a constitution.
>
> Excited by the prospect of getting into power and in their haste to reach there, ... [however], the leadership aspirants appear to have convinced themselves that apart from themselves and their interest groups, no one else is capable of questioning the validity of their proposals ...
>
> Many of us Ghanaians have no political leadership ambitions, but we are keenly concerned about the constitution by which the leadership aspirants will seek to protect or toy with our lives.

Other questions that remained were the lifting of the ban on political parties and the proposal to hold a referendum to approve the constitution. The 'leadership aspirants' were eager for the former, but curiously shy about the latter. Lifting the ban, of course, would immediately return the initiative to the hands of the impatient politicians. They would be free to wheel out the old party machinery and mobilise sufficient mass support at public rallies to make the country ungovernable, until they got their way. No matter how it had arrived in power, however, the PNDC was still the government of the day and as such it had a responsibility to maintain stability in the country. As Christian Aggrey put it 'the formation of political parties before their roles, functions and conduct have been clarified is putting the cart before the horse'. Rawlings put it in his characteristic style, to lift the ban now would be 'an insult to the intelligence' of the people's representatives at the Consultative Assembly.

The grounds for opposing a referendum on the constitution were even more dubious. On the one hand, a referendum would apparently be time-wasting and costly; on the other hand, in a 'predominantly illiterate society' like Ghana's, one should not expect that many people would understand a complex document like a constitution. Those who hold the latter view have little understanding of the real purpose of a democratic constitution as the custodian of the people's rights.

At the end of July 1991 Dr S.K.B.Asante's Constitutional Committee published its proposals for the consideration of the Consultative Assembly. It is a fine and thoughtful document, based upon consideration of a wide range of other constitutions, from Ghana and abroad, and taking for its guidance an underlying principle of the 31 December revolution, namely, respect for the poorest and most vulnerable individual in the state. Thus under the section on human rights and personal freedom, it went beyond the normal abstract freedoms of every Bill of Rights and added an economic dimension, reiterating the oft-quoted saying that 'freedom of expression is meaningless to a person with an empty stomach'. It was concerned not just with how to run a Parliament, but with the whole social and economic future of the nation.

In an interview published in *The Mirror* on Saturday 25 May 1991, a prominent former politician characterised the futility and shallowness of the old style of party political conflict when he said:

> The ban on politics must be lifted this year but after the NAM conference [early in September] because we need a united front to welcome the delegates and it will be a shame while the delegates are here if we shall be throwing mud at each other.

If that was still all that party politics meant to certain former politicians, then some people had learned little from the bitter experience of the past!

Ghanaian politics needed to be freed from the scourge of the 'winner-takes-all', confrontational politics which had discredited the parliamentarians of the country's previous three republics. It was with this in mind that the Asante Committee came down firmly in favour of some form of proportional representation. Government by consensus, which this system would promote, was far more in keeping with the Ghanaian national character and traditional way of doing things.

At the time of writing, the Consultative Assembly has just begun its sittings. By the time this book is published, it will have completed its deliberations. If it follows the guiding principles of the Asante Committee's proposals, then it will come up with a worthy and lasting document, fit to provide the sort of political stability which Ghana so badly needs and so deserves.

On 26 August 1991 Chairman Rawlings opened the proceedings of the Consultative Assembly. In doing so, he set out a timetable for a return to full constitutional government. The Assembly's proposed constitution would be put to an internationally-monitored referendum in January or February 1992 and, assuming it were approved, elections could be expected to be held in the third quarter of 1992. In the event, the process was delayed by three months as the Assembly needed more time to complete its deliberations.

In August 1983, in an interview with the *Ghanaian Times,* Jerry Rawlings had said:

> If in ten years time every Ghanaian can live decently in modest comfort, taking a full share of responsibility for the well-being of the nation and participating in the shaping of its destiny, then I hope that by then I can find time to live for myself.

By the third quarter of 1991, very many Ghanaians were still not living in modest comfort. They were, however, beginning to take a moderate share of responsibility for the well-being of their nation. Through wide participation in the Consultative Assembly, they were, in however small a way, participating in the shaping of the nation's destiny.

Ghanaians have achieved a great deal under PNDC rule and many have taken their inspiration from the personality and integrity of its Chairman, Jerry Rawlings. A sound financial basis has been laid for real economic development. The producers of the country's wealth are still seriously disadvantaged by an unfair international balance of world trade, but at least they are not having their efforts further undermined by widespread incompetence and corruption. Through the relentless drive of the Head of State, and in an effort to prove the legitimacy of their 'government of the people', ministers of this unelected government have striven far harder and with greater honesty and dedication than many of their predecessors. A greater degree of integrity and accountability has been restored to government.

There have been numerous faults in the PNDC's record of government, as there are in that of any government. The greatest single fault of the PNDC has been its cavalier attitude to the personal freedom of the individual. It has used and abused the detention laws, often on very little evidence or on the basis that someone has dared to challenge the direction or the legitimacy of 'the revolution'. In doing so the PNDC has lost the trust of many people and alienated scores of potential allies.

What remains for Ghanaians to do now is to build upon the undoubted gains of the past decade and to prove their personal and political maturity by forgiving the errors of the past – on all sides – and working towards that stable, fair and more prosperous future that is now possible. In these critical times of political turmoil on the continent, Ghanaians have the ability and the opportunity to regain their stature as 'the Black Star of Africa' and lead the way forward to a new democracy.

Select Bibliography

In addition to a wide range of official publications, the following is a short list of the newspapers, books and articles most widely consulted in the research for this book:

Newspapers and periodicals

People's Daily Graphic (formerly *Daily Graphic*)
Ghanaian Times
The Mirror
The Pioneer
The Spectator
The Catholic Herald
Free Press
West Africa
Africa Confidential

Books and articles

Kofi Nyidevu Awoonor, *Ghana, a political history* (Sedco and Woeli, Accra, 1990).

David Birmingham, *Kwame Nkrumah* (Cardinal, London, 1990).

Naomi Chazan, *An Anatomy of Ghanaian Politics* (Westview, Colorado, 1983).

E. Gyimah-Boadi (ed), *Ghana under Rawlings* (forthcoming, CODESRIA, London), including chapters by Joseph Ayee, Kweku Folson, Takyiwaa Manu, Kwame Ninsin, E. Gyimah-Boadi and A. Essuman-Johnson.

Emmanuel Hansen and Paul Collins, 'The army, the state, and the "Rawlings Revolution" in Ghana,' *African Affairs*, Volume 79, January 1980.

Richard Jeffries, 'Ghana: the political economy of personal rule,' in Donal B. Cruise O'Brien, John Dunn and Richard Rathbone (eds), *Contemporary West African States* (CUP, Cambridge, 1989).

Ebenezer Mireku, *Which Way Ghana?* (Asuo Peabo, Accra, 1991).

K.A.Ninsin and F.K.Drah (eds) *The Search for Democracy in Ghana* (Asempa, Accra, 1987).

Kwame Nkrumah, *Dark Days in Ghana* (Panaf, London, 1968).

Barbara E. Okeke, *4 June: A Revolution Betrayed* (Ikenga, Enugu, 1982).

Emil Rado, 'Notes towards a political economy of Ghana today,' *African Affairs*, Volume 85, October 1986.

J.J.Rawlings, *Selected Speeches*, Volumes 1 to 8 (Ministry of Information, Accra, 1982–1989).

Donald I. Ray, *Ghana* (Pinter, London, 1986).

Kojo Yankah, *The Trial of J.J. Rawlings* (Ghana Publishing Corporation, Accra, 1987).

Emmanuel Doe Ziorklui, *Ghana: Nkrumah to Rawlings*, Volume 1 (Em-zed, Accra, 1988).

Index